Richard Madeley

This book belongs to

Jenny

My star sign is

Sagittarius

My favourite colour is

Green

My favourite pop star is

_____

The thing I hate most is

_____

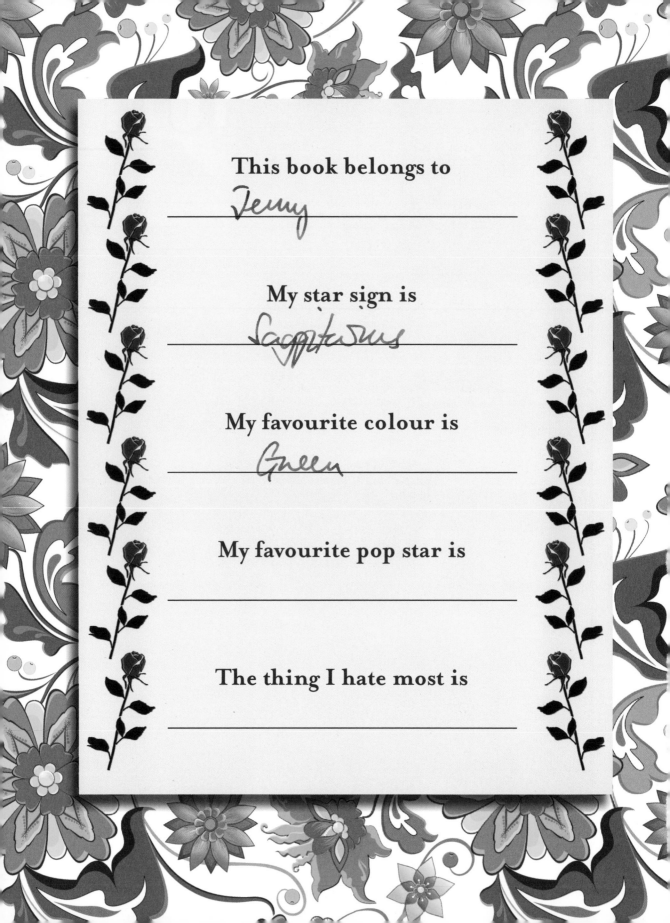

Wendy

The Bumper Book of Fun for Women of a Certain Age

Jenny Éclair
Judith Holder

HODDER &
STOUGHTON

First published in Great Britain in 2008 by Hodder & Stoughton
An Hachette Livre UK company.

A CIP catalogue record for this title is available from the British Library
ISBN UK Edition 978 0 340 97756 9   ISBN ANZ Edition 978 0 340 92005 3

Designed by unreal, 20 Rugby Street, London, WC1N 3QZ
Printed and bound in Italy by Graphicom Srl

Hodder & Stoughton policy is to use papers that are natural, renewable and recyclable products and made from wood grown in
sustainable forests. The logging and manufacturing processes are expected to conform to the environmental regulations of the
country of origin.

Hodder & Stoughton Ltd, 338 Euston Road, London NW1 3BH   www.hodder.co.uk

Wendy

Dedicated to
middle-aged women
everywhere —
without whom,
the world would spin
off its axis and run
out of milk.

ALSO BY
JENNY ÉCLAIR

HAVING A
LOVELY TIME
CAMBERWELL
BEAUTY

ALSO BY
JUDITH HOLDER

GRUMPY
OLD WOMEN
IT'S (NOT) GRIM
UP NORTH
DIARY OF A
GRUMPY OLD
WOMAN
GRUMPY OLD
HOLIDAYS: THE
OFFICIAL
HANDBOOK

ALSO BY
JENNY ÉCLAIR
AND
JUDITH HOLDER

GRUMPY OLD
COUPLES:
MEN ARE FROM
MARS.

WOMEN HAVE
JUST GOT BACK
FROM TESCO'S

Contents

COLUMNISTS

POISON IVAN
STYLE GURU

Will the Emperor Nero of Fashion give you the thumbs up or the thumbs down in our 'What your life style choices say about you?' quizzes.

Born an only child to an ageing Russian Princess, Ivan was horrified to find out that his mother was in fact Pauline Clegg from Ormskirk and that for his entire life she had been 'putting on a funny voice'.

DR RUDOLF CLERC
MD, PHD, MPHIL, INST PSCHY, (HON)

Discusses mid-life hobby choices and their serious side effects.

Trained in Krakov at the Empirical School of Psychosomatic and Psychodramatic Psychology and Physiology. He wears very studious glasses, and has a lot of very erudite-looking books behind his desk so that people who come to see or interview him are impressed.

Doctor or quack? It's up to you – either read what he has to say – or disregard him as a complete charlatan.

JUDITH HOLDER AND JENNY ÉCLAIR

Writers, co-editors and brains behind **Wendy**, Judith Holder and Jenny Éclair have been working together ever since they were thrown out of a quilting and rag-rug class for being 'rowdy and silly'.

GLENDA & DEREK
AGONY AUNT AND UNCLE

Got a problem? Let our resident Agony Aunt and Uncle, Derek and Glenda Parnell sort you out.

Glenda and Derek have been married for 30 years and have learnt to tolerate each other. They have gained an international reputation for their guidance on marital and emotional problems of any kind.

ZANDRA WIENERSCHNIT-BLACK
DELVES INTO YOUR NIGHT-TIME SUBCONSCIOUS

Zandra trained in Selbstverwircklichun-gian counter-transference techniques (a very advanced form of something) and uses dream analysis as a clinical observation technique. Her own recurring dream of being a cinema usherette in the 1950s is something she is currently working on. Shrink or witch? All we can say is that it's a good job it's not the Middle Ages, they'd have burnt her at the stake!

letters page

Hi girls, thank you so much for all your letters and emails. We really love sharing your thoughts, even if some of your correspondence has to be handed over to the relevant authorities. Just remember the letter of the week wins a Pifco hairdryer*.

Dear Wendy,

Although I am only fifteen I often turn to you for advice about fashion and beauty. Imagine how thrilled I was the other day when someone mistook me for a forty-three-year-old divorcée.

Bibi (I call myself Brenda), Cartridge, West Yorks

Congratulations Brenda.
I bet your mother's really pleased and not worried at all.

Dear Wendy

I did embarrass myself the other day. I wanted to make myself some new net curtains and so I went to my local department store and asked for three metres of muslim, to which the young girl said, 'Well actually I'm only five foot two and I'm Hindu!'

Marion Bostock Smith, Selly Oak (but the nice bit up by the park), Birmingham

As long as we can all laugh at these things, eh?

*Unfortunately this week we couldn't decide which letter was the best so *you're all winners* (although none of you will be receiving a hairdryer).

Dear Wendy,

I refer to your June issue and fashion feature titled 'Styles for the Womanly Woman-Shaped'. Like many Wendy readers I am indeed a womanly-sized 22 – my husband of 28 years adores my curves and likes a woman he can 'get hold of', but I am sorry to say the stockists of some of your suggested underwear and strapless tops do not go up to my size. I think you should know because other readers of a similar shape and size to me will have been wasting time trying to order stock to no avail.

Yours grumpily
Naomi Pilmer, Melton Mowbray

Dear Naomi,
There is a limit to how much we can do for lardy pants like you. Size 22, strapless tops – good heavens woman, what are you thinking?

Dear Wendy,

A really funny thing happened to me on the way to the supermarket. As soon as I remember what it was I shall write and let you know.

Love Val, Tewkesbury

Dear Val,
That would be great, but please, if you are going to write to us again, please remember to put a stamp on the envelope. Why not try emailing, it's much cheaper.

Dear Wendy,

Here is a snap of my little grand-daughter, Coco (her mother's idea). She is only three years old and as bright as a button, and she has two grannies. There's me, who she calls little grandma, and her maternal grandma who she calls fat grandma. Don't kiddies say the funniest things?

Yours truly,
Henrietta, Taverstock

Dear Henrietta,
We're only printing this so everyone you know
will realise what a horrible person you are.
PS We are donating your fee to anti-bullying
organisation. So kind of you.

Dear Wendy,

The other day I locked myself out of the house. I tried to climb in through the lavatory window but got stuck and my smug neighbour called the fire brigade to get me out. Mind you, I had the last laugh because as soon as the dishy fireman saw me, he asked me out on a date. How's about that for karma?

Meredith Lamhurst, Stockton on Tees

Dear Meredith,
So you've found a tubby-loving firemen. Well, lucky
you! Send him round here when you've had enough
of him and just remember that although some men
find the larger lady attractive, obesity can lead to
heart disease and diabetes. You may also want to
think about some therapy for what is evidently a
nasty case of early onset Attention Seeking.

Dear Wendy,

Last night I was on my bike going home carrying all my essay papers for marking (I'm a school teacher) when I hit a pedestrian in the road and to my annoyance, all the papers fell out of my basket. Imagine my amazement when the young man who I mowed down got up, dusted himself off, apologised profusely and then introduced himself as none other than John Travolta.

Alison Drury,
Telford

Dear Alison,
We've received letters from you in the past, haven't
we? Last time it was Jack Nicholson who accidentally
picked up your smoked trout in the fishmongers. What
a glamorous life you lead up there in Telford!

Dear Wendy,

I just wanted to let you know that even though I am a man and certainly not gay, I really enjoy reading your magazine. My fave bits are the love stories and the pin ups – especially the newsreaders as I think they're all really handsome and clever. Please, please, please could you do a full-length pin up of the Sky News political correspondent Peter Spencer or as I call him, the silver-haired fox.

Gavin Notts, Brighton

Dear Gavin,
We'll do our best. And in the meantime, may we
suggest you grow a moustache, not because you're
gay, but just for fun.

Dear Wendy,

I'm writing to ask if any of your readers would know of the whereabouts of a Glynis Bamford? Only I leant her a two-person bivouac back in 1997 and I've not heard from her since

Stanley Trepass, Herne Hill

Well, ladies... ?

CAN'T REMEMBER HOW OLD YOU ARE?

Find out in this simple quiz. Saves having to dig out your birth certificate!

Do you find yourself accidentally singing all the words to 'Billy, don't be a Hero'? Have you heard yourself saying, 'Gosh, aren't blueberries expensive this time of year?' Have you got flares in your wardrobe that are older than Cat Deeley? Whether you're twentysomething, thirtysomething, fortysomething or beyond, we'll help you find out how old you really are.

What was the last thing you said?
A) What day is it today?
B) Turn it down
C) One espresso macchiato, please
D) Safe, wicked

Your Doctor Who is...
A) William Hartnell
B) Jon Pertwee
C) Peter Davison
D) Paul McGann

What sort of bicycle did you have when you were growing up?
A) A penny farthing
B) A Raleigh
C) A chopper
D) One of those new-fangled scooters

What time do you go to bed?
A) Around 9.30 with a good book
B) Around 10.30 with a good malt whisky
C) Around 11.30 with a good man
D) Haven't been to bed yet this week

What have you got pierced?
A) Nothing
B) Ears
C) Ears several times
D) Ears, tongue, belly button and clitoris

What sort of sandwiches did you have in your school packed lunch?
A) Powdered egg
B) Spam
C) Cheese and tomato
D) Guacamole

Your favourite sports personality is…
A) Pat Smythe
B) Olga Korbut
C) Gazza
D) Becks

At school, did your teacher write with…
A) A quill?
B) Chalk on a blackboard?
C) Marker pen on a white board?
D) Power point presentation?

Your favourite fictional character is…
A) Muffin the Mule
B) Pinky and/or Perky
C) Bagpuss
D) Pikachu

The hairdo that you had when you were fifteen was…
A) A simple bob with an Alice band that was backcombed at weekends
B) A disastrous poodle perm
C) Farrah flicks
D) Pink

How's your pubic hair?
A) Thinning as we speak
B) Bit frizzy and grey round the edges but you keep it under control with the nail scissors now and then
C) A neat landing strip, thank you very much
D) What pubic hair? You've gone for the full Hollywood

What's your recreational drug of choice?
A) A nice cup of tea
B) The occasional Nytol and a glass of port
C) Ecstasy in a field about fifteen years ago
D) MDMA – look it up

Answers

Mostly As – over 55
Well done you for actually being able to read this. You went to school with God, that's how old you are. Mind yourself on the stairs now.

Mostly Bs – 40 plus
Still continent but getting a bit forgetful.

Mostly Cs – under 40
Still capable of conceiving. It's downhill from now on so if you do want that baby you had better hurry up.

Mostly Ds – 20-30
Young enough to go clubbing and still live with your mum and dad. Make sure you haven't got an STD.

At last, incontrovertible proof that there aren't enough hours in a day! No wonder a good woman's work is never done! We haven't got the time!

the RUN OFF YOUR FEET pie chart

Nagging – 1hr 15min

Supermarket shopping – 1hr 11min

Afternoon nap – *45min*

General anxiety – *17hrs 35min*

Worrying about weight – *9hrs*

Moaning about ironing – *2hrs 39min*

Actual ironing – *4min*

Texting – *9min*

Taking things back – *2hrs 50min*

Drinking white wine – *1hr 30min*

Watching soaps *1hr 30min* and daytime telly – *6hrs*

Thinking about what to cook – *56min*

Supermarket shopping – *1hr 11min*

Going back to supermarket to get what you forgot – *19min*

Cooking – *27min*

Sex, thinking about sex – *0.00008secs*

Thinking about sex with Daniel Craig – *14.5min*

Writing list for cleaner – *3min*

Lying on the sofa – *2hrs 25min*

Nagging – *1hr 15min*

Looking for glasses – *11min*

Reading – *9min*

Sleeping – *4hrs 7min*

Pacing round the kitchen checking all the windows are locked – *7min*

Tossing and turning – *1hr 14min*

Sleeping fitfully – *3hrs 6min*

Having a bath – *19min*

Hair and make- up/shaving/plucking/cutting corns etc – *22min*

Deciding to go to the gym – *6min*

Changing your mind about the gym – *1min*

Total = 55hrs 13min and 8.00008 seconds

Worrying about weight - 9hrs

Cooking - 27min

Shaving/plucking etc - 22min

So it adds up to more than 24 hours but that's the point! It feels like more than 24 hours! And people wonder why we are tetchy/furious/ready to kill/ if someone fails to put the milk back in the fridge.

THESE BOOTS ARE MADE FOR WALKING

I bought the ticket from the little newsagent next to the dry-cleaner's. I wouldn't have even been there had Gareth not wanted his shirts doing express.

'Really, Julia, you are stupid. You might have known I'd have needed the dress shirt for the Taverners' do on Sunday.'

Well, I didn't know. I couldn't remember him telling me, but then, as Gareth says, I've got a head like a sieve.

Gareth tells me lots of things. He doesn't actually talk to me, he imparts information or gives me orders but we never really have a chat. I chat to my girlfriends and to my cleaning lady. I think I like Moira the cleaning lady best of all my friends because she is funny and wise and, unlike most of my other friends, doesn't pretend to like Gareth.

'...Moira smokes cheap cigarettes that "stink the house out"...'

Moira is Scottish and probably the only person I know apart from Gareth who still smokes. Gareth smokes in the house, but Moira must smoke outside. This is because, according to Gareth, Moira smokes cheap cigarettes that 'stink the house out', unlike his cigars, of course.

Moira must be my age. She works because she is divorced and her mother, who has Alzheimer's, is in a home in Dumfries, which needs paying for, and two of her grandchildren are living with her because their dad, Moira's son, is on heroin.

I've met Moira's grandchildren. They are sweet freckle-faced girls of six and eight. Gareth would go mad if he knew about Moira's son; he'd be convinced he'd be round using Moira's keys to burgle us blind. Well, how could he? Moira's son is in prison.

No one has it easy, all Moira wants is to set up her own cleaning agency – 'Moira's Marvel's', she said she'd call it. 'We'd have pink overalls, Julia, we'd all have pink overalls.'

Moira comes on a Monday and a Friday. Sometimes I miss her on a Friday because I have to play bridge. I have to play bridge because that's what Gareth expects, so on Fridays I play bridge, I meet the girls for coffee on Wednesday, I volunteer in the hospital on Tuesday and on Monday I do the big supermarket shop.

I haven't really worked since I got married. Gareth didn't want me to, he wanted me to have his children and look after him. Fortunately I managed to give him two sons, which kept him happy for a while.

I love my children but they are men very much like their father and I find their wives brittle and distant, although very well groomed.

I am waiting for grandchildren. I want a baby to knit for and a toddler to take to the swings, but even if it does happen my children live too far away for me to

have much input. They will have nannies and au pairs and I will be an annoying interference. Oh well.

I live in a very nice house, everyone says so, but it's very big for the two of us and Gareth is out such a lot.

Gareth is a successful businessman. He is something in the City, which I have never understood, and apart from his job he sits on the boards of various committees and charities. Any old excuse to drink brandy, that's what I'd say if I had the courage, which obviously, I don't.

Gareth is a bully; he has bullied me for thirty years. I am nearly fifty, I should be able to stand up for myself, but every time I try he puts me down.

Moira tells me I should get a divorce. To be honest, I would very much like to, but I'm too scared to ask. This is what he's done to me. Gareth has never hit me, but he has made me do a lot of things that I haven't wanted to do, and I know there have been other women, because he told me so.

I bought the ticket two days before my fiftieth birthday. The next day I realised what the ticket meant, so when the day of my birthday actually dawned I knew what I was going to do next.

Gareth gave me golf clubs. I didn't want golf clubs; they were the last thing I wanted. He also bought me a lifetime membership for the club, and to celebrate that fact we would be dining at the golf club that very evening.

The boys sent flowers and one of their wives rang – the one that calls me Julie, not Julia. To get my own back I called her Tasmin. She said, 'Actually it's Tamsin.' I said 'And I am Julia, good day.'

Moira came over to clean, but because it was my birthday we had coffee together. She bought me my favourite Crabtree & Evelyn soaps and gave me the cards the girls had drawn. When it was time for her to have a cigarette, I made her smoke it in the kitchen. 'But,' she said, 'what about Gareth?' and I said 'Stuff Gareth.' I had the ticket in my boot, it gave me the confidence to say and do what I liked.

Moira and I talked for ages. We talked for so long she didn't have time to hoover Gareth's study. 'Just leave it,' I said and we laughed. When she left I gave her an overnight bag to take back to hers. Everything was falling into place.

I dressed nicely for dinner but I kept the boots on, I felt it was safer.

Gareth had kept his driver on for the evening. Marty has been with Gareth's company for the past seven years or so. I don't think he likes Gareth, he gives me sympathetic looks in the rear-view mirror when Gareth is at his most pompous, which is practically every journey.

Gareth picked us up at 7.30 p.m. and we were at the golf club by eight. Marty said he'd be waiting

in the car park. 'Should be bored and ready to go around ten thirty,' barked Gareth.

We had a drink in the bar first. Gareth talked to a lot of middle-aged men with red faces, drinking spirits. I had a gin and tonic that I didn't really want, I fancied some champagne. 'The old girl's fifty,' Gareth kept yelling, 'Bout time I traded her in for a younger model,' and he winked at the barmaid behind the counter and she gave him a look back that I'd seen women give him before.

We sat down to eat at 8.45. When the wine waiter came I asked for a bottle of champagne. 'Well,' said Gareth, 'I'm not sure that's a very good idea. I fancied a bottle of red because I'm going to have a steak.'

'Well,' I said, 'it's my birthday and I'm having champagne.'

'Yes, madam,' said the waiter and he was back in two ticks with nice bottle of Krug on ice.

Normally when we go out for dinner Gareth tells me what I should have. This is because certain foods turn his stomach – like fish – whilst other things are too fattening for a woman who is a borderline size 16 (like pâté). This will frequently leave me with the choice of melon – which is a bit dull.

I ordered the pâté followed by the roast monkfish.

'What are you doing?' asked Gareth.

I said, 'Pleasing myself.'

He looked a bit confused.

I have to say I enjoyed my meal. Poor Gareth got a duff steak and he didn't like his artichoke soup. Well, I could have told him that, he's not the vegetable type.

We didn't talk much, he just droned on about how golf would do me good and mostly I just nodded my head.

I waited until I finished my pudding. 'Are you sure you want a pudding?' Gareth had asked.

'Yes,' I'd replied, 'I am certain.'

Then, whilst we were having coffee, I told him.

I said, 'Listen to me, Gareth, I am leaving you. I'm not asking you for a divorce but I am telling you that I don't care if I ever see you again. I've had enough and I'm not coming home with you. You can huff and puff until you are purple in the face. I don't love you, you don't love me, what's more, you make me unhappy. I am staying somewhere else tonight. Once I'm safely there I shall send Marty back for you. I suggest you join your cronies in the bar. No doubt you'll be seeing even more of them from now on. Goodbye, Gareth.'

And I picked up my handbag and walked out, my £3.2 million-pound winning lottery ticket safely zipped up in my boots.

THE END

'...it's my birthday and I'm having champagne.'

WHAT YOUR HAT

All of us need a hat for hiding a bad-hair life,
but what does your choice of titfer say about you? POISON IVAN,
our resident gay design-Nazi, gives you the low down.

THE BOBBLE HAT

You are the practical dog-walking type. I bet your skin is really dry and flaky so why not try a little moisturiser before your face peels off entirely? You're the type of woman who really believes that looks don't matter, good job in your case. If you were a meal you'd be a really dried-up shepherd's pie. Try to be a bit more adventurous; maybe pop a bit of lipstick on now and again, and just remember there are younger prettier women out there and some of them will be quite happy to break up your marriage. Of course, 1 in 300 bobble hat wearers are really pretty girls who are studying art at Glasgow university. These are the bobble hat funksta brigade, not to be confused with the dog walkers.

THE BERET

Ooh la la, where are we off to? Paris on the Eurostar, or just to the shops? Either way, who cares, it's nice to make the effort. The beret is a fashion classic and suitable for most face shapes. Whatever you do, do not make Frank Spencer impressions whilst wearing it; the trick is to pretend you were too young to watch *Some Mother's Do Ave 'Em*. Don't be tempted to overdo the French motif. Even if you have got quite a heavy moustache, the beret is enough, so resist accessorising with a string of onions around your neck.

SAYS ABOUT YOU

THE SHOWY-OFF HAT

Look at you, lady (which is precisely why you bought the thing)! The Showy-Offy hat is commonly worn by ex-wives at any event where the ex-husband might be. It's a female power thing – the bigger the hat, the more furious the female. Veils are great for hiding faces that are distorted by disappointment and revenge, a great disguise for the lady who doesn't want to be seen grinding her teeth in public. Also worn by desperate types at Ascot, who would do anything to get their pictures in the *Mail on Sunday*. Sad.

THE NOVELTY HAT

Namely something made out of felt that looks like an upside-down flower pot, or that has long yellow plaits attached, or anything Timmy Mallet might have worn. Be very careful, the novelty hat can be a sign of deep depression. On the one hand you're saying, 'Look at my hat, aren't I the fun-loving gal?' but underneath, you're screaming. Why not go and have a chat with your GP? 76% of novelty hat wearers are on anti-depressants.

THE TURBAN

Aren't we the exotic one? Either that or you've just got out of the bath. Women who wear turbans beyond the boudoir might have a touch of the Norma Desmond from *Sunset Boulevard* syndrome. There's a bit of the diva devil in you and you're probably a bit demanding and attention-seeking; some of your friends think you're a bit of a bitch.

How to be
Dance Aware

A lot of middle-aged women let themselves down on the dance floor; some are a downright disgrace. The problem is, when you get to our age there is precious little that makes you blush. In fact, you don't really give a monkey's what people think of you, which is very useful indeed when you are ranting or raving at young girls making fools of themselves on hen nights, but is less of an asset on the dance floor.

Here at **Wendy** we feel it our duty to point out some of the dance moves that can let you down when it comes to that family wedding, office disco or charity ball. The danger zone normally arrives after the first glass of champagne, the three white wines that come quickly after, and the misplaced decision to move on to red. Sooner or later the DJ will put 'I Will Survive' on, and in a sudden act of over enthusiasm, a busty rush to the dance floor ensues. This is when things can go 'Over the Top'.

At a wedding, the 'Over the Top' moment usually coincides with all the young people who were dancing when you got up on the dance floor going back to their tables or returning to the bar to continue chatting one another up. You are left with the groovy grannies, or better yet, doing the twist with all the toddlers.

Golly! That will hurt in the morning.

Dancing Do's

1 Do practise a few simple moves in front of the mirror – perhaps get a friend to videotape you so that you can make sure you're not doing anything that will make young people sneer.

2 Do remind yourself of any current or past injuries. If for example you've ever had your knee in a brace it might be wise to avoid moves that put pressure on this particular area.

3 Do remember that not everyone wants to join in; do not drag a shy sixteen-year-old boy out of his chair and force him to 'boogie' with you – young people are very easily embarrassed and he might be psychologically scarred for life.

Dancing No-No's

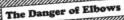

The Danger of Elbows

Pistol Shooting

This would be sexy in a minxy sort of way if you were twenty-four and were at a Cowboys and Indians fancy dress – but you're not, it's the Ladies Circle AGM and you promised to run the tombola.

Get the Moves!

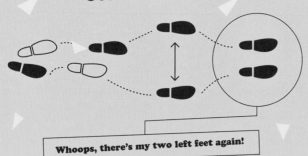

Whoops, there's my two left feet again!

Too Much Elbow Action

We can all get carried away with a heady feeling of enthusiasm when we think that we are recapturing our youth. Sometimes you don't know your own strength; someone who has been on the receiving end of your powerful elbow thrusting will let your tires down as an act of revenge.

Hitch Hiking

This was all the rage in 1968. Your daughter can do it and make it look ironic and knowing, but when you do it, you just look old and mad. Oh well, at least it serves as a public warning about the dangers of picking up strangers by the side of the road.

Pogo or Rave Attempts

You've seen the young people doing it and think it's going to make you look happening. It doesn't, and anyway you don't have the bra for it. If you are not wearing a bra or just have a strapless on, don't be surprised if cracks appear in the walls around you.

I need a ride

Correct use of hitchhiking

The Twist

An acceptable dance – it shows a sense of fun and impressive physical agility. Do watch what you twist to: it is good for Chubby Checker or Billy J Kramer, but absolutely not to M People. **NB** Anyone who attempts to twist down to the floor only has themselves to blame if it ends in a trip to casualty/bandages/Ralgex.

Keep this number handy!

999

Scottish Dancing

OK, so you did it at school and can still do a passable attempt at the 'dashing sergeant'. However, because you went to an all-girls school you only know the man's moves, and this could cause chaos – might be better to sit it out.

Inappropriate

Smooching

Fine and really rather touching as long as it doesn't involve tongues. On the other hand how likely is that – who are we kidding?

No Tongues

Remember

Be dance appropriate – for example barn dancing does not lend itself to the Rolling Stones or Ian Dury. Equally, dancing like a punk and jumping up and down and spitting is not advisable at your friend Miriam's 50th hoe-down.

NO TONGUES

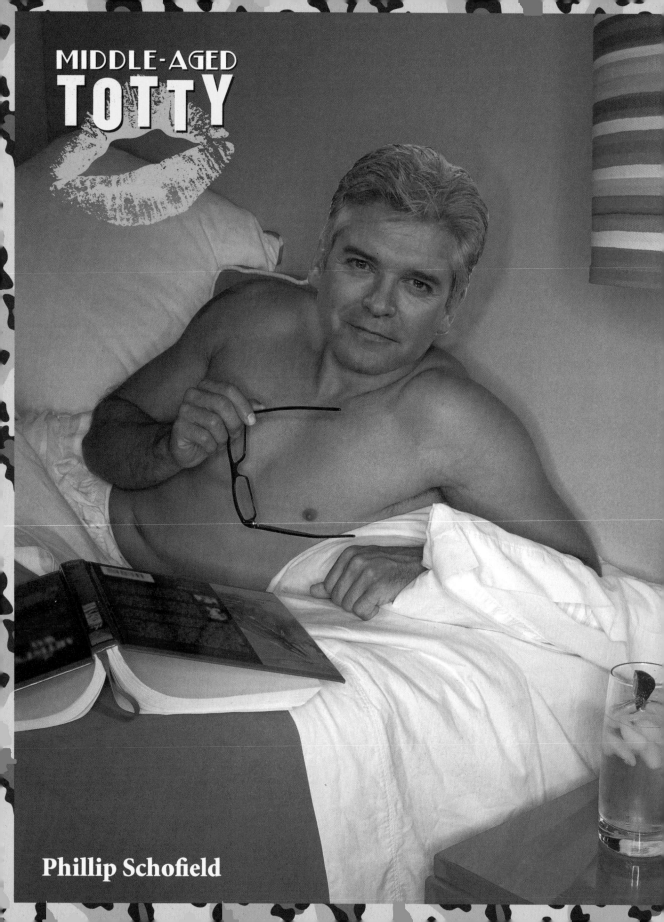

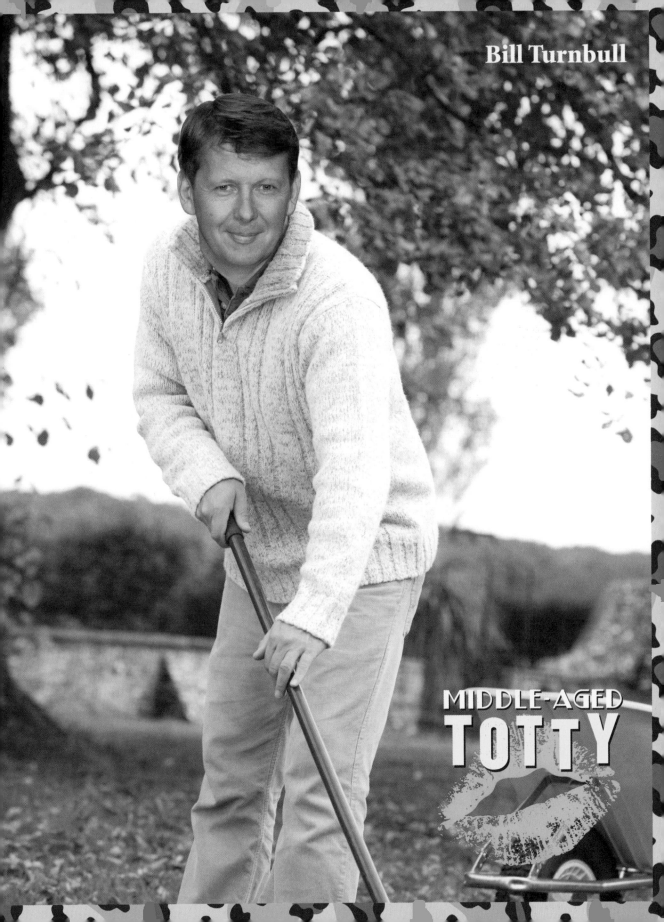

Bill Turnbull

MIDDLE-AGED
TOTTY

Tangled String
QUIZ

WHICH TOP GEAR PRESENTER DO YOU FANCY THE MOST? Pick a tangled string – A, B, C or D – to find which car bore drives you wild.

JEREMY C

Likes: A A Gill and
Cowboy Boots
(but isn't gay)

Dislikes: Eco-warriors,
Vegetarians,
Piers Morgan and Buses

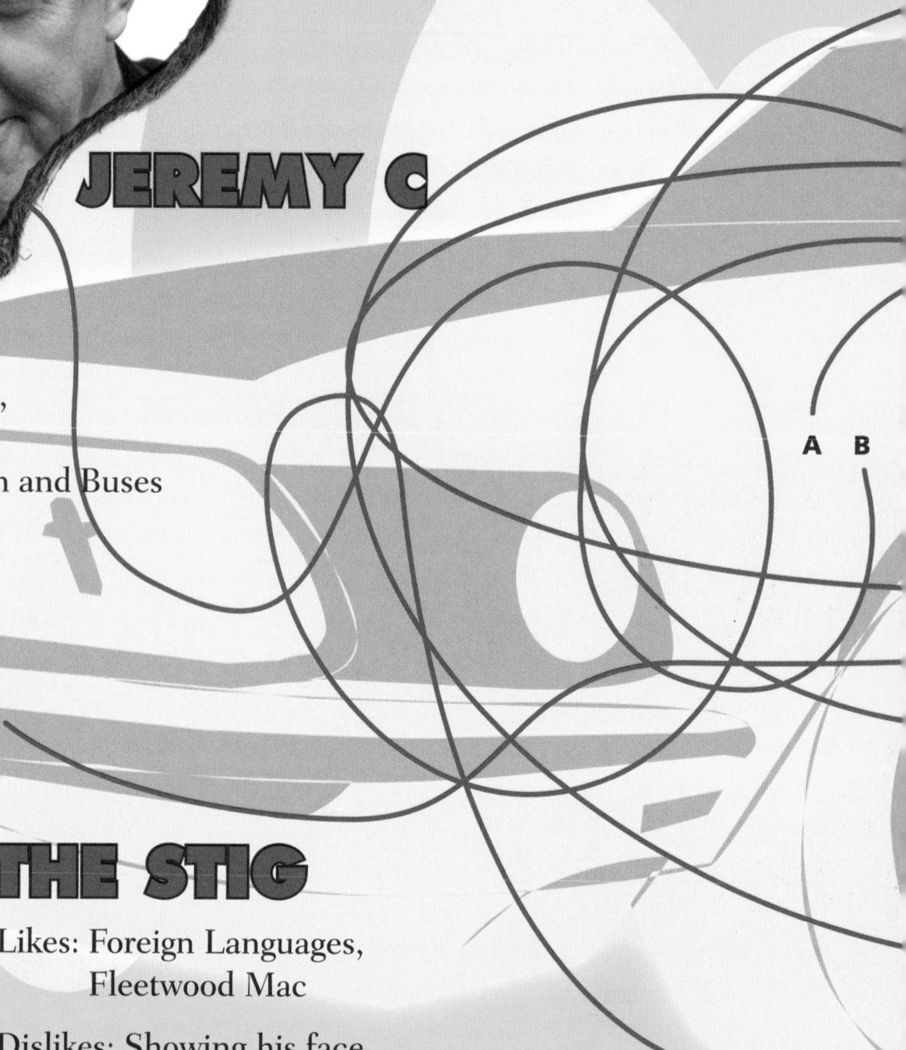

A B

THE STIG

Likes: Foreign Languages,
Fleetwood Mac

Dislikes: Showing his face

RICHARD HAMMOND

Likes: Seeds & Grain
Dislikes: Drag racing

C D

JAMES MAY

Likes: Driving slowly
Dislikes: Shampoo

JOB INTERVIEW?
HOW NOT TO IMPRESS

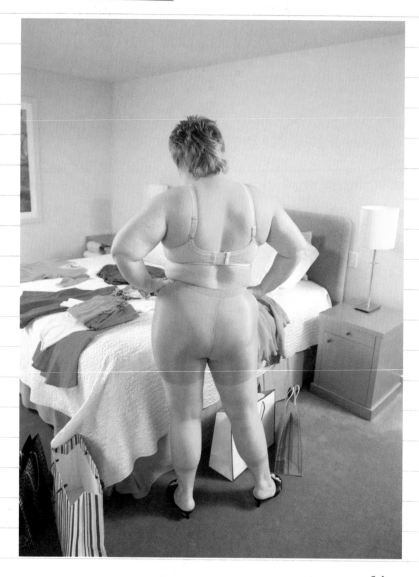

We've all been there. At some point in our lives we've all been offered an interview for something really important and have needed to come out smelling like roses.

But making a good impression needs time, energy and planning, so make sure you don't leave it too late. The last person they want to meet is the real you!

HOW NOT TO MAKE A GOOD IMPRESSION

GREY ROOTS – Whatever you do make sure you've been to the hairdresser. If you've run out of time either cover the grey with a black or brown felt-tip pen, or, rather than have two tone hair, give in to the grey. After all, grey is the new blonde.

HAIR ONLY STRAIGHTENED ON ONE SIDE (THE OTHER SIDE AU NATUREL AND REALLY FRIZZY) – Whoopsadaisy, if you've only had time to straighten your hair on one side, hide it.

FROWN LINES – You don't want him to think you're too stressy for the job, so quickly cut yourself a fringe! If that doesn't look right, wrap a bandage around the offending area and tell them you are recovering from a skiing accident. They will be impressed.

MOUSTACHE – We all know hormones can do terrible things, but that's no reason to resort to the razor. Ask for some electrolysis for your birthday... or wear a yashmack.

FEATHERED LIPSTICK – Use a lip liner to avoid this unfortunate look. If the grooves between your lips and nose are really deep, keep your lipstick light – a red lipstick that's spread can look like you've just had a nosebleed, which might lead them to think you have either been fighting or taking drugs.

MUESLI IN TEETH – The 'I've just chewed my way out of a quarry' is so not a good look. Floss, floss and floss again, but not during the interview – pulling strings of clumped up bits of food out of your mouth is unprofessional in an interview situation.

CHIN WHISKERS – Pluck, pluck and pluck again. However, as above, not during the interview. Whatever you do, don't ask your potential boss if he'd mind getting the 'big wiry one' that you can't quite get a grip on.

GARISH SILVER EYESHADOW – More suitable for the disco a muted shade would be much more flattering. This is a look which screams I went out on the pull last night and never made it home.

DOUBLE CHIN – If you know you've got a job interview in two weeks' time, don't eat for the fortnight beforehand. If that doesn't work, either tilt your head back for the whole interview, or wear a polo neck.

DANDRUFF ON THE SHOULDERS – Use Vosene, the strongly medicated anti-dandruff shampoo. They'll be able to smell your problem but they won't be able to see it.

A BEAUTY-ON-A-BUDGET *Special*

Here at *Wendy* we fully appreciate the importance of beauty, but we also know that many of us are hard-bitten sceptics who would like to give those silly women who work on cosmetics counters a big black bruise on their arm for selling overpriced beauty products whilst wearing a silly white lab coat and pretending it's some sort of cutting-edge science.

Why spend a fortune on make up and skin care when so many essential beauty must-haves can be found in your own home and garage? It's true, everything you need is either in the cupboard or the fridge or lurking at the bottom of his toolbox.

WE ALL KNOW THAT MASHED-UP AVOCADOS ARE GOOD FOR THE SKIN – but if you haven't got any guacamole, try hummus. Remove from the face after fifteen minutes with either warm water and cotton wool, or some pitta bread.

JAZZ UP FADING GINGER LOCKS with a squirt of tomato ketchup in with your conditioner, works a treat and economical too.

RUN OUT OF HAIR DYE and exposing embarrassing grey roots? Soy sauce is a marvellous temporary solution; simply apply with cotton wool and avoid the rain!

FED UP OF PAYING FANCY SHOP PRICES? Why not make a DIY hard skin exfoliator? Simply glue a sheet of sandpaper around a match box and abracadabra! Your very own handbag sized hard skin remover.

LARD – the indispensable beautifier – adds shine to dull and lifeless hair. Fab for smoothing dry elbows and making lips more lustrous. Regular lard massages into stiff joints can prevent embarrassing creaking.

GRAVY GRANULES smeared on legs and arms gives that lovely sun kissed look (but you must ex foliate first).

FELT TIP PENS make marvellous eye shadows and lipsticks, though staining your lips with blackcurrant jam (apply with a cotton bud or finger) also works a treat, particularly if you are after a more goth look.

INSTEAD OF LIP GLOSS use a tiny amount of furniture polish (that beeswax stuff in a jar is nice. Don't use Mr Sheen spray, you'll get in a mess). Neutral coloured shoe polish also does the trick; however be careful not to lick your lips as they might be a bit poisonous.

RUB A SLICE of beetroot onto your cheeks to add a healthy glow.

MAKE YOUR OWN EYELINER by burning a match and using the burnt charcoal bit at the end to effect a sexy smoky look.

PRETEND YOU'RE OLDER THAN YOU ARE. That way you get more compliments which will in turn boost your self-esteem.

PLAIN, RATHER THAN SELF RAISING FLOUR is a great alternative to face powder, especially for those with a pale complexion (for those with a slightly faun colouring go for wholemeal flour). If you haven't got a spare powder puff, apply with a bap cut in half.

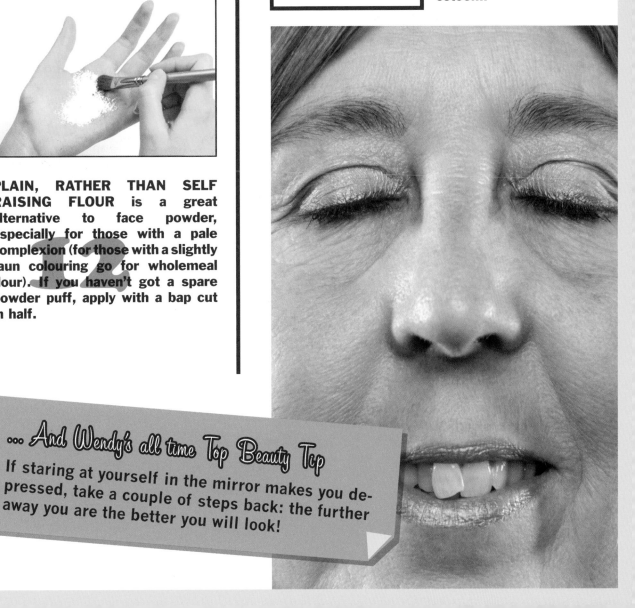

... *And Wendy's all time Top Beauty Tip*
If staring at yourself in the mirror makes you depressed, take a couple of steps back: the further away you are the better you will look!

IF YOU CAN'T BE BOTHERED TO TRY TO LOOK YOUNGER, YOU CAN CONCENTRATE ON HOW TO <u>FEEL</u> 15 AGAIN...

We're all getting on and however hard we try and however much money we spend, it's really tricky to fight the ravages of time (unless of course you're Sharon Osbourne and you've got the number of the world's best plastic surgeon on speed dial). For the rest of us, it's a case of soldiering on and smiling through. But as we all know, it's not what's on the outside that counts; beauty comes from within, so if you want to look younger, you need to feel younger. Here's how:

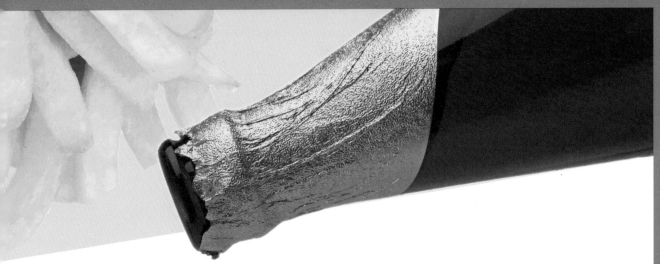

Could the key to looking younger, be feeling younger? *Feeling* 15 again is really easy, all you need to do is follow some of these simply *Wendy* rules and hey presto, mentally you're back in the Lower-Fifth.

- ♥ Fall out with your parents.
- ♥ Slam a bedroom door.
- ♥ Overpluck your eyebrows.
- ♥ Snog your best mate's boyfriend (or husband as he is now) and get him to give you a love-bite.
- ♥ Eat chips on a night bus.
- ♥ Listen to the same sad song over and over and over again.
- ♥ Have a fag in a phone box (if you can find one).

- ♥ Drink cider out of the bottle (but don't make a habit out of it).
- ♥ Wag off work and spend the day in an amusement arcade.
- ♥ Borrow your sister's best cardigan without telling her.
- ♥ Pretend your pillow is someone you really fancy.

- ♥ Nick something from Woolworths.
- ♥ Get bubble gum in your hair.
- ♥ Give yourself a tiny homemade tattoo like a star – but make sure it's hidden by your watchstrap.
- ♥ Go out without a coat and lie about where you've been.

Stand Here

Another Sneaky Way to Look Younger
Surround Yourself With Older Pals

Why colours matter

Before you buy anything make sure it's in a colour that suits you. Here's a quick guide to making the right choice:

YELLOW

Only for those with Mediterranean skin tones, so make sure you have some Italian or Spanish blood before you go wasting your money. If you're not sure, ask your mum.

Spanish Blood?
Then yellow is safe to wear. Olé!

PINK & RED

Very flattering on those with fair complexions, but if you suffer from broken veins around your nose, it's probably best to avoid maroon.

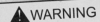

⚠ **WARNING**

 | AVOID MAROON

GREEN

Not for the superstitious. Every time you wear it you will think something bad is going to happen and now and again it will. Remember, crashing the car into a bollard whilst wearing a green jacket does not mean it was the jacket's fault. You just can't drive, or see very well for that matter.

Woman in brown: Clearly European

BROWN

Hmm, it's a bit dull isn't it? But then maybe that's a reflection of your personality? For some reason European women look sophisticated and chic in chocolate and camel hues, us English birds just look a bit drab.

TAUPE
& OTHER STRING AND PUTTY-COLOURED SHADES

ighly sophisticated, but not for those with
allow skin tones – you will look like you
re coming down with something. The rule
f thumb here is, if your skin is the colour
f putty, avoid puttyish shades. There are
ome colours that look better on a wall
han on you.

...some colour shades look better on a wall than on you.

BLUE

Suits most people, though electric blue needs
careful handling, especially if it's an electric
blue jacket with shoulder pads. Amazingly,
there are some items of clothing that only
Christine Hamilton can get away with.

WHITE

Again, better suited to those with darker
skin tones (ask your parents if you've got
any Egyptian ancestors). Also a waste of
time unless you have incredibly dainty
eating habits. Best for foreign women who
never eat spaghetti bolognaise.

BLACK

Suits everyone, regardless of skin tone, and
is a particular favourite with those who are
feeling chunky. Black is very forgiving and the
best colour to spill gravy down

*The incredible slimming
effect of black*

ORANGE

Only mad people wear orange.

shoes shoes shoes

For men shoes are functional – something to keep their feet dry, kick a tyre with or shake their athlete's foot powder in....

But for women shoes are – well, how shall we put it? – one of the things that make life worth living. Yes, they might be a touch more expensive than a bar of chocolate, but they will last you longer than three stops on the bus and even if you put on four stone, you should still be able to squeeze them on to your bulging trotters.

A woman's choice of shoes is a form of self-expression. When a woman chooses a pair of shoes she is saying a lot about how she feels, about what she wants and doesn't want out of a relationship. For example, Nicole Kidman always wore heels when she was married to Tom Cruise, just to remind him what a shorty he was. A good man – a gay man, realistically – can find out an awful lot about a woman, just by looking at her shoes:

- If a woman only has three pairs of shoes or likes sensible leather lace-ups she may be a lesbian.
- A woman who wears a navy loafer with a pair of brown nylon tights is most likely an unmarried school teacher (physics probably).
- A bossy middle-aged woman who wears a thigh-length patent leather boot may well be a dominatrix (or an off duty traffic warden).

Unfortunately, some women let their love affair with shoes get out of proportion. Love shoes, yes, but there is a time and a place for every shoe, and if your children are walking barefoot whilst you teeter along in Jimmy Choos, you've probably got the balance a bit wrong.

SHOES TO WEAR IN COURT

This, by the way, is not what your mother means when she talks about a court shoe. Court shoes should have a modest but understated heel – think policewoman on her day off. A silly high heel could backfire badly in court, especially if you are claiming damages due to a tripping hazard. Much better to go for the shabby trainer and the sympathy vote instead.

SHOES TO WEAR TO PARENT/TEACHER EVENINGS

Spiky stilettos in classy chocolate leather – these shoes send out 'don't mess with me' signals, forcing the headmistress to back off from any impending disciplinary action she might have been plotting for your darling. Considering the damage these heels could inflict upon the parquet flooring, she's not likely to keep you waiting. Good, you'll be in the pub having a gin and slim-line by 8pm.

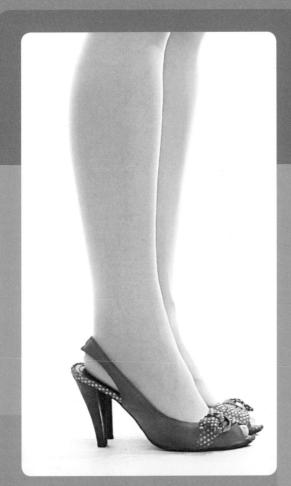

SHOES FOR PULLING

Peep toes are good but only if you have had a pedicure and don't pick your toenails at night. A medium-size heel is appropriate but anything over the top will make you look very common indeed if you have to resort to a heel plaster to carry the wines over. Obviously avoid white pulling shoes – people will assume you are a prostitute/Polish pop star.

SHOES FOR IRONING

No woman really needs a special pair of ironing shoes, but men don't need to know that. All you need say is that your doctor suggested that a pair of good ironing shoes would prevent your spine from crumbling as you iron his shirts. He will be so consumed by guilt that you might be able to get some Stacking the Dishwasher shoes out of him as well. The fool!

SHOES FOR WEDDINGS

Avoid the perils of over-matching. If your dress and jacket are peach, don't in any circumstance wear peach shoes – you'll look like a flamingo. This may be taking attention-seeking too far.

SHOES FOR A KID'S PARTY

It's important to have a pair of easily-cleaned patent party shoes that can be wiped clean of squashed birthday cake, jelly and sick. Only a very foolish woman wears a suede or soft leather shoe to a child's party.

SHOES FOR THE RAIN

It's only when you are standing in the pouring rain wearing a pair of non-waterproof shoes and your tights have started to squelch that you realise why those shoe shops try to sell you protector spray or wax. And you thought they were just trying to squeeze more money out of you. Maybe next time you won't be so sneery.

WELLIES

Wellies with themed chocolates or strawberries or jolly flower power patterns are okay if you live somewhere unfashionable like in the North, but definitely not if you find yourself (by mistake) at Glastonbury or have to visit your teenagers at Uni. They are so last summer.

BOOTS

Tricky – especially finding a pair that you can get zipped up at the calf without causing a lack of circulation that leads to amputation. Although... this would cut down on shoe bills and you could team up with another amputee to buy shoes jointly.

SHOES FOR HOSPITAL VISITS

Avoid lace ups that squeak, unless you want the patients to pass you the bedpans when you walk through the wards.

If you really can't wear heels anymore you are going to have to buy some stylish flatties in lots of different colours and jazzy designs. But beware the attention-seeking route, which looks more like a desperate cry for help.

However painful your bunions, just remember it's a very bad idea to buy beige-coloured shoes from a pharmacy. It signifies the sad fact that you have given up on foot fashion for life. Ditto shoes from the back of the *Sunday Express* magazine.

It's a good idea to check your shoes regularly for dog poo, especially if there seems to be a funny smell wherever you go.

Three pairs of shoes is not enough, thirty pairs of shoes is a bit silly and greedy.

Shoe Tips

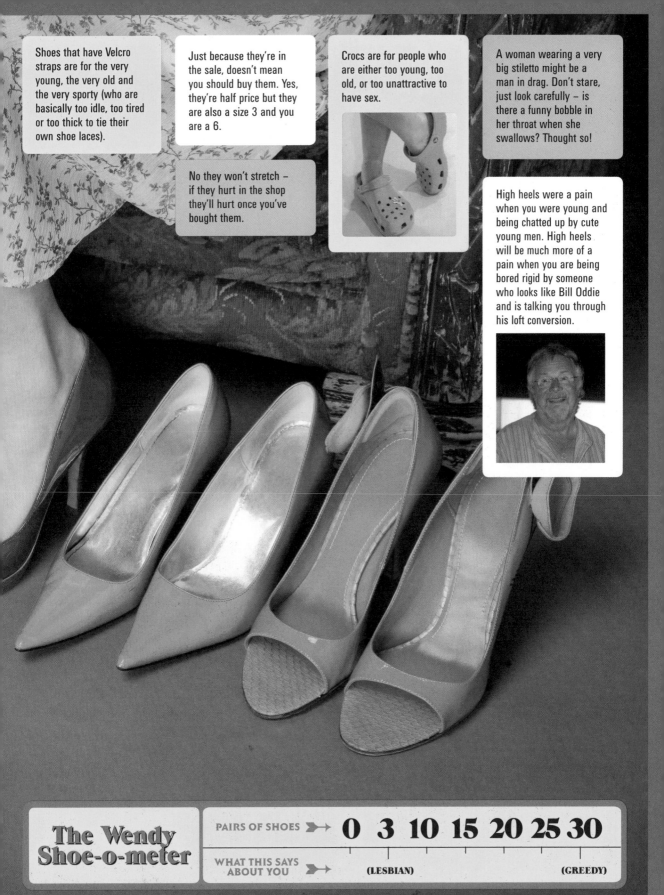

Shoes that have Velcro straps are for the very young, the very old and the very sporty (who are basically too idle, too tired or too thick to tie their own shoe laces).

Just because they're in the sale, doesn't mean you should buy them. Yes, they're half price but they are also a size 3 and you are a 6.

Crocs are for people who are either too young, too old, or too unattractive to have sex.

A woman wearing a very big stiletto might be a man in drag. Don't stare, just look carefully – is there a funny bobble in her throat when she swallows? Thought so!

No they won't stretch – if they hurt in the shop they'll hurt once you've bought them.

High heels were a pain when you were young and being chatted up by cute young men. High heels will be much more of a pain when you are being bored rigid by someone who looks like Bill Oddie and is talking you through his loft conversion.

The Wendy Shoe-o-meter

PAIRS OF SHOES →	0	3	10	15	20	25	30
WHAT THIS SAYS ABOUT YOU →		(LESBIAN)					(GREEDY)

ARE YOU TURNING INTO A WITCH?

Wendy readers everywhere will be aware that some of us turn into witches as we get older, blending in distressingly well at Halloween parties or just being evil, manipulative and plain bloody-minded. If you doubt this, then take a look at your mother-in-law and consider how easily you too could turn into her. Do this quiz to discover how likely you are to turn into a witch yourself...

When someone fails to give you good service in a shop, say a dozy Saturday girl, do you...

A) Smile sweetly and sympathise with how tricky their job must be, even if you don't really think that?
B) Make such a scene that the supervisor comes over and gives her a good telling off?
C) Casually find out when her next shift is and plot a way to get her the sack?

When (very) old ladies dawdle on the pavement, or don't indicate when they are about to change direction, do you...

A) Offer to do their shopping for them because they must find it so hard, especially in the bad weather?
B) Make a great big huffy-puffy fuss in the street but pretend you only have her interests at heart... You'd hate her to have a fall!
C) Take it out with a good hard kick at her tartan shopping trolley – it nearly snagged your tights – and then pretend it was an accident?

When your mother-in-law comes to stay, is your instant reaction to...

A) Spruce up the spare room and get some nice spring flowers for her bedside table? After all, she only comes to stay once a year and she means well (and will leave the kids some money).
B) Pretend you have deadlines to meet at work so that you can spend as much possible out of the house while she is there? You caught her opening the airing cupboard and having a good poke around last time.
C) Encourage her to admire her son's new vegetable patch? The steps down to it are very wobbly and if she's not careful she might slip and be indisposed for months.

When someone spits on the pavement leaving a horrible gobby mess, do you...

A) Give him that look you can do which used to scare the kids when they were (very) small?
B) Shout after them and tell them how perfectly unsociable it is to spit on pavements and how would they like it if you spat on their living room carpet?
C) Get one of the lollipop sticks out of your bag and scoop some up and take it to the local police station? With the DNA databank these days, forensics might be able to track him down.

Mostly As: Reason and age tells us that you will obviously one day turn into a witch. For now you are able to pass for a normal/really-quite-civilised sort of woman. Make the most of it. Skip more, swing a guitar from your arm, and buy a dirndl and a big hat.

Mostly Bs: You (sort of) mean well and can just about manage to keep your hideously horrible evil side under wraps. This can't and won't last for ever, so you need to make sure you cover your tracks: never write down any bitter horrible thoughts, ones that you wouldn't like to be read out in court. Always a good maxim for life.

Mostly Cs: It's uncanny. You are a witch. Are toads and rodents inexplicably drawn to you and hop into your handbag? Has Channel 4 approached you to feature in a new series on extreme witches? Has someone given you a cauldron for Christmas? All or any of these things could well be happening to you soon. The point is you need to embrace it. Ideally, run the tray bake stall at the WI or sort the charity shop stuff as it comes in. All the bargains and the one-upmanship are yours for the taking.

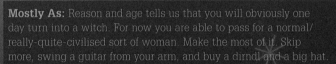

A-Z
OF
THE MENOPAUSE

Are you experiencing the change of life?
Hot flushes more and more common?
Losing your hair?
Don't faff about having horrid blood tests, just
take a quick look at our A-Z of the menopause and
see if it reminds you of anyone?

A is for '**Anyone fancy some fresh air?**'
The menopausal matron is forever having to cool off.

B is for '**Beg Pardon**'. She's increasingly hard of hearing but her experience has taught that it's rude to say 'what?'

C C is for '**Cheerio!**'. All of a sudden her language has fallen into a pre-second world-war vortex.

D is for '**Do I look as old as her?**' A query she will repeat with ever increasing plaintiveness. Be very careful how you respond.

E is for '**Eggs don't agree with me**'. Actually nothing agrees with her, including the family.

F is for '**F*ck**'. Swearing is acceptable now and again — especially in the car.

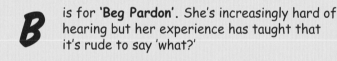

G is for '**Good game, good game**' said in a Bruce Forsythe impression followed by embarrassed laughter as she realises what she has just done.

H is for 'Have you kept the receipt?'
Taking things back is her new religion.

I is for 'I'm not really in the mood'.
If she's not in the mood, don't push it.

J is for 'Just one more chocolate then take them away from me.'
Don't you dare.

K is for Kiss.
Unfortunately, no one seems that interested.

L is for 'Look here young man,'
said with nostrils flaring.

M is for Mood swings, Memory loss and err, something else.

N is for Nothing new about flared trousers.

O is for Old.

P is for Peking. Beijing indeed.

Q is for 'Quick, take the photo.
I can't pull my tummy in any longer.'

R is for 'Run up and get me my glasses will you, darling girl.'

S is for 'So you didn't really remember our anniversary.'

T is for for Tupperware. You can never have enough.

U is for 'Use a hanky!'

V is for Vicks Vapour Rub –
a favourite embrocation.

W is for 'What was I going to say?'

X is for Xtra large.

Y is for 'You'll need a coat if you're going out.'

Z is for a little Ziz.

10 THINGS
THAT ARE GUARANTEED TO MAKE US GO GRRRRRRRRRR

1. A broken dishwasher that decides it's broken only when it is chockablock with dirty dishes.

2. A splinter that you can feel but can't see to get out, not even with a magnifying glass.

3. Bin men who spread the contents of your bin up and down your garden path.

4. An inexplicably cold bath.

5. A fry-up with no tomato ketchup.

6. A great big grease splodge on your new satin blouse.

7. Falling over in the supermarket for no reason whatsoever, so you can't even sue.

8. Non pooper-scoopers – don't pretend you didn't see that dog of yours do that great big steaming pile of poo.

9. Your boss flirting with the new young temp – silly old fool.

10. Forgetting to watch your favourite telly programme.

A SPECIAL ON DEPRESSION

Even the jolliest of us will feel a bit BLUE now and again. Sometimes it's hard to put your finger on just what's wrong and it becomes more a case of not feeling yourself, being under the weather or a bit below par.

The thing about depression is that it can hit you at any time, anywhere. One minute you can be having a perfectly nice time, perhaps hosting a dinner party, laughing and joking with your guests, and then all of a sudden you wish everyone would just shut up and go home!

So let's do a quick medical check up to see if you're afflicted.

Answer these simple questions and find out whether you're just a bit moody or quite frankly teetering on the edge of a massive nervous breakdown.

ARE YOU DEPRESSED?

1) Have you ground all the enamel off your teeth?

2) Do you feel ready for bed as soon as you've got up?

3) Is it some time since you changed your nightie?

4) Have you stopped bothering to open the curtains?

5) Is eating anything apart from tubs of ice cream in bed too much effort?

6) Are you avoiding all your friends in case they say something about the fact that you can't be bothered to comb your hair?

7) Is your hair a bit matted?

8) Does rocking backwards and forwards offer you a crumb of comfort?

9) Have you set fire to your dressing gown recently?

10) Are those animal noises coming out of your mouth?

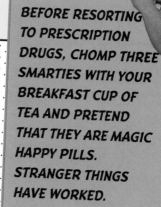

Under 3 Yeses
You're just a bit hacked off. All you really need to do is pull yourself together, woman.

3-6 Yeses
You're properly depressed and you've got every right to go completely berserk when people tell you to 'cheer up'.

6-8 Yeses
You shouldn't be left alone in the kitchen, not with all those sharp knives.

Over 8 Yeses
You don't need a doctor to tell you you've lost it. All you need to do is try and find 'it' before people start tapping their heads when they mention your name.

BEFORE RESORTING TO PRESCRIPTION DRUGS, CHOMP THREE SMARTIES WITH YOUR BREAKFAST CUP OF TEA AND PRETEND THAT THEY ARE MAGIC HAPPY PILLS. STRANGER THINGS HAVE WORKED.

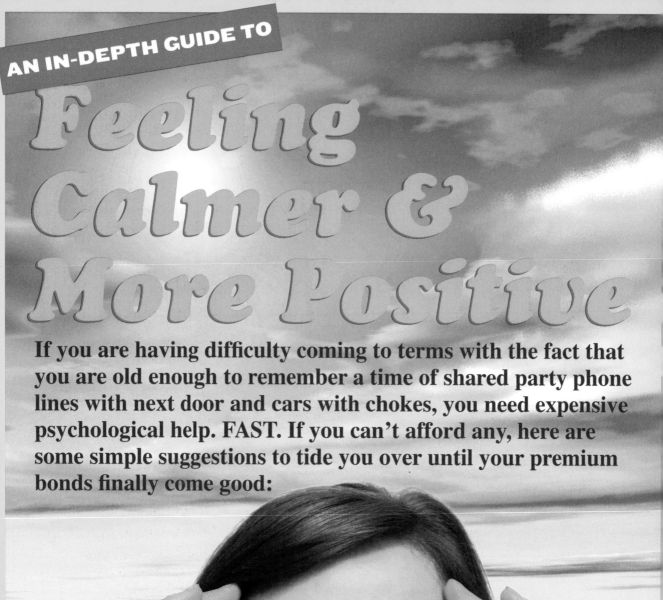

Feeling Calmer & More Positive

If you are having difficulty coming to terms with the fact that you are old enough to remember a time of shared party phone lines with next door and cars with chokes, you need expensive psychological help. FAST. If you can't afford any, here are some simple suggestions to tide you over until your premium bonds finally come good:

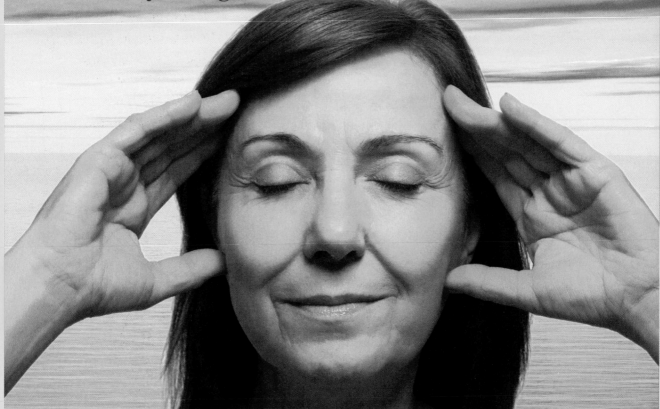

Get out of the house

Make sure you've checked that you locked the door, otherwise your anxiety levels will go through the roof.

Go to a big department store

Somewhere like John Lewis will make you feel like there is calm and order in an otherwise mad world. Particularly comforting is the bed linen department – nothing as soothing as lots of beautifully made beds.

Feel in control of things

Buy some batteries, in all shapes and sizes, as well as some candles and Sellotape. Having these things in the house (make sure you put them somewhere you know you will be able to find them) will give you a deep sense of calm.

Get some exercise

We all know that exercise releases endorphins that make us feel better, but not all of us have got swanky gym memberships and are mentally strong enough to face a swim at the local turd-infested pool. So why not get a bit of a sweat up by clearing out the attic. Or just start with the cutlery drawer. Clean and tidy cutlery is the key to Zen-like fulfilment.

Do something that will make you feel good later

Send some money to a really worthy charity. A fiver to Great Ormond Street is guaranteed to make you feel like Mother Teresa for weeks to come.

Get some fresh air

Gather up all the mismatched socks and beyond-hope pants in the house and make a bonfire in the back garden. You might be tempted to bake a potato in the embers, but we can't guarantee the flavour.

Do something you've been meaning to do for ages

Take all those bottles you've been meaning to recycle down to the recycling place, Take the duvet to be dry-cleaned, get those boots re-heeled, clean the barbecue and creosote the fence. Go on.
Then afterwards, treat yourself with…

Really satisfying sex

It's almost as rewarding as unclogging the filter and pump in the pond. So why not make a day of it and do both!

So there you go. Our guide to feeling calmer and more positive without resorting to reading any silly self-help books or, God forbid, buying some daft crystals.

Dreamy Days

Dreamy
Days

Wendy's Short Stories

TURNING BACK THE HANDS OF TIME

Do you ever feel that if you could turn the clock back you would? I do. For starters, I wouldn't have married Jim. Don't get me wrong: my husband is a good man. I should count myself lucky; Jim doesn't gamble or drink and God knows, if he tried to hit me I'd have him on his back before he knew what had happened.

Jim has no vices: he is neat and tidy and orderly, he knows where the documents for the household insurance are and when the car needs a new MOT. Jim is sensible and he wears a suit to work. Sometimes when he comes home from a busy day I'd like him to take his suit off, put on something a bit more casual, but somehow Jim looks all wrong

in jeans – he's the sort of man who really only looks right in a tie. Good old Jim, his sandy hair is falling out and he is becoming increasingly long-sighted – all that sitting at a desk counting numbers, I suppose. Jim is an accountant, always has been, always will be.

I need Jim. Without him I would have done something daft, gone to live in Spain, bred horses. I certainly wouldn't be living in this pin-neat house on the outskirts of Edgbaston.

Without Jim I would drink too much, spend too much and forget that I am a woman of forty-five, that I have responsibilities, that it doesn't do to forget oneself and go a bit bonkers now and again.

That is why I need Jim. The truth is that I have a tendency – correction – I *had* a tendency to go a little bonkers now and again. These days I am a very tame version of what I used to be. I am a primary schoolteacher, and every day twenty small children call me by my name, reminding me over and over again that I am Mrs Carmichael and it's too late to be anyone else.

I have made my bed (Jim insists) and I'm lying in it and it's very comfortable but sometimes I could scream with boredom.

Before I settled down and became Mrs Carmichael I was Patty Ferris. Patty Ferris was good at art and mad on clothes and boys. I was a teenager in the seventies. I had fun, perhaps a bit too much fun. I lived near Blackpool, where there were hundreds of bars and clubs on my doorstep. I was a sociable girl, and in 1979 my mother's hair went grey. 'You'll be the death of me,' she would say as I staggered in hours after I was meant to be home. 'Be careful, Patricia, I don't want you getting into trouble.'

And somehow I didn't: I went off to Manchester to study art. I was living away from home and I was finally free, free to do whatever I liked – which I did.

I lived in a shared house in Didsbury where people came and went. I had finished college but I was still living like a student; there didn't seem to be any reason to grow up. I waited tables to pay the rent, painted at home and danced through the night. I drank a lot and took a few too many drugs and never thought about my future. Until I met Greg.

Greg was in a band. He moved in to the flat above mine and while I painted, he wrote songs and we'd bump into each other on the stairs and I'd want to run my fingers through his hair.

Greg had a girlfriend who was a model; he had a girlfriend who was American; he had a girlfriend who was the daughter of a diplomat.

Greg was the lead singer in the band, the front man. I used to go and see him gig, and every now and then he'd give me a lift home after in the transit van that his mate Freddie drove.

I fell in love with Greg. It was easy: he was gorgeous and funny and talented and great in bed as it turned out. So I loved Greg and Greg loved me but he also loved Julie and Soraya and Annabelle, and I tried very hard not to mind. But I did. I minded even more when the band got successful and there were

> *'I fell in love with Greg.*
> *It was easy.'*

even more girls hanging around, each one younger and prettier than the last. I was twenty-four and already feeling past it.

He didn't tell me he was going. I had realised the flat was empty but I didn't know he'd gone to the States. Then one day I read about his move in a music magazine. I knew he was going to make it, and I knew that he was going to make it without me.

I stopped painting; I stopped doing anything. I drank a lot and smoked like a chimney. I couldn't eat, I felt sick and didn't bother getting dressed.

One day I heard music from Greg's old flat, I raced up the stairs – but an unfamiliar face answered the door, a nice face, a bit freckly, with glasses, nothing special. 'I'm Jim,' he said.

Jim has been looking after me ever since we first met. For him it was love at first sight, something he'd never previously believed in. For me, he was the solution to everything that was out of control in my life.

Of course, I never stopped seeing Greg, how could I? He was everywhere, in the papers on the television. He's on his third wife now and I doubt he even remembers me. He is rich and famous, and I am a married mother of one.

Which reminds me, Jed should be home soon. I've made him his favourite: spaghetti bolognaise. He won't stay long, you can see him getting bored. Jim tries, of course, but he has no idea how to talk to him.

Jed's moved on, his life gets bigger as mine gets smaller – my son, my long-limbed, blue-eyed boy. He's in a band, of course, the lead singer, the front man, and he is so like his father that I can't be sure that Jim hasn't guessed. But as I said, my husband is a good man: I should count myself lucky.

THE END

Just remember we are all reaching that time of life when the doctor is going to strip us off and weigh us. Good bras and pants are an investment against the potential embarrassment of standing on the surgery scales wearing something that even a rat would reject for nest-building purposes.

If you're not comfortable in a thong, don't wear one; there is nothing worse than the sight of a middle-aged woman constantly trying to pick her thong out of her bottom crack, you will look like you have threadworms and are trying to have a sly scratch.

Beware hold ups – they don't.

Don't whatever you do borrow your partner's Y-fronts. It is wrong.

Wendy's GUIDE TO UNDERWEAR

The thing about being a fully paid-up middle-aged *Wendy* reader is that by now you will have settled into your 'underwear for life' mode. For some of us that means buying thirty pairs of knickers for three quid from Chorley market, and for others it means lingerie purchased from a special shop with a discreet doorbell.

Now and again we need to be ruthless with ourselves, we need to go through our knicker drawer and decide what we can wear again, and what is only suitable for cleaning out the cooker.

Why not get your bra fitted properly at a department store? You might think you're a 34A when in fact you're a 38F and the reason why you've been having chest pains is because you're bra is too tight.

For those of you with the smaller bosom, why not try chicken fillets? Or if they're a bit pricey, why not pop in a couple of salmon fishcakes? Just remember to keep an eye on the sell-by dates. Oddly-sized bosoms are a bit like oddly-sized feet, a real nuisance! But as long as it doesn't affect your balance, you can disguise the problem by carrying a clipboard and pretending to be doing a survey.

Trampolining in a strapless bra may lead to innocent bystanders taking legal action for post-traumatic stress.

PANTS: The first basic rule that governs underwear: every woman needs five pairs of everyday pants, two pairs of black lace, two pairs of white lace and two pairs of satin 'ooh lala's' for high days and holidays.

If you've got a horrible next-door neighbour who is really competitive, it's worth buying some really fancy pants just to hang on the washing line. She will be intrigued as to how you squeeze into these little wisps of nylon and lace. Meanwhile, dry your big girls pants on a clothes horse in front of the fire.

BRAS: Your average certain-ager, unless she's a pole dancer or something saucy, needs eight bras. Three everyday, one sports, one halter neck, one strapless and two fancy.

HERE'S A HANDY HINT: YOU SHOULD CHUCK YOUR BRA AWAY WHEN THE PADDING LOOKS LIKE IT'S BEEN CHEWED BY A DOG AND THE WIRES ARE HANGING OUT AS IF THE THING IS ABOUT TO DETONATE.

WENDY SAYS

Wendy's Diet Pull Out Special

All of us are obsessed by our weight. It's a madness, but the vast majority of us think we're too fat, which is why 95% of the female population over the age of eighteen is either on a diet, thinking about going on a diet, or sneaking a biscuit out of the tin, eating it and then feeling worse than if they just ran over someone's cat.

What's your guilty pleasure?

— V —

For years we have been encouraged to eat sensibly and exercise – but we all know that doesn't work, so for those who have nowhere else to turn, we have decided to create the ultimate fad diet, gathering together all the really stupid fads that have been knocking around for the past thirty years and merging them into one scientifically proven, Super Fad diet.

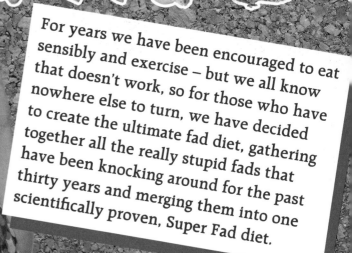

SUPER FAD DIET

Monday

BREAKFAST
Large portion of anything you don't like, i.e. semolina or huge number of roll mop herrings.

LUNCH
You will feel so sick after breakfast that you won't be able to stomach lunch. Great, you have saved 400 calories. Either put these in your calorie savings bank to spend on Twixs at the end of the week or blow it in the pub on a stomach calming gin and slimline tonic. Allow yourself three crisps from your thin friend's pack of cheese and onion.

MID AFTERNOON SNACK
Two chewable Rennies.

SUPPER
Go to a ridiculously expensive restaurant – the only thing you will be able to afford is the starter – go for the soup, if there's a choice, ask the waiter which one is the most like dishwater and choose that – it will be called 'consommé' which is French for dirty water.

Tuesday

BREAKFAST
Porridge made with water – essentially gruel as given to prison inmates in the last century. Afterwards, go outside and break up some rocks, chain-gang style. If you're wearing manacles this will burn off loads of calories.

LUNCH
Some mussels bought from a dodgy van – make sure you force open the ones that are closed – with any luck you will get a bout of food poisoning. It might be cheating, but who cares?

SUPPER
Nothing but hot water with a squeeze of lemon. Hoorah, you did find the dodgy mussel!

Wednesday

BREAKFAST
Cabbage Soup.

LUNCH
Cabbage Soup.

SUPPER
Cabbage Soup and some Immodium. Remember changing soiled sheets is great for burning up calories.

Thursday

BREAKFAST
Dry cereal eaten with chopsticks. By the time you've eaten a quarter of it, you will be two hours late for work.

LUNCH
Cancelled, as due to late arrival – you have to work though lunch break.

SUPPER
Half a grapefruit mashed up with a small tin of tuna in brine. So revolting it could almost put you off food for life.

Friday
ATKINS DAY – HOORAY!!

BREAKFAST
Fried eggs and bacon.

LUNCH
Steak and mushrooms with a creamy peppercorn sauce.

SUPPER
An E.C.G. and overnight stay at the local hospital.

Saturday

HOSPITAL BREAKFAST
Can of Coke from vending machine and a Twix whilst waiting to be discharged.

LUNCH
A handful of dried fruit, figs and apricots – it's been a while since you've been to the lavatory.

SUPPER
Two 'crisp break' pizzas – pizza's dull cousin. Smear a couple of crisp breads with tomato paste, add some ham, onion and rocket. It's almost like the real thing, but not.

Sunday

BREAKFAST
Strawberry flavour Slimfast milkshake.

LUNCH
Chocolate flavour Slimfast milkshake.

SUPPER
Chicken, veg and gravy flavour Slimfast milkshake (three new flavours – choose from roast chicken, lamb or beef, all specially blended with semi-skimmed milk to provide you with a nutritious replacement Sunday dinner savoury milky shake drink). Two sticks of sugar free gum for dessert (to take the taste away).

Well done
You've lasted a week on our scientifically proven Super Fad diet. Now all you need to do is repeat the whole process every week for the next six months.

Remember: this diet will work even better if you skip the occasional meal and take a laxative.

A WENDY Special
THE TRUTH ABOUT FOOD ALLERGIES

Over the past few years allergies have become all the rage and even if you're not actually allergic to anything, it's fashionable to pretend that you are. Here are some suggestions of food groups you can pretend to be 'intolerant' to:

- **Wheat**
- **Gluten**
- **Yeast**
- **Lactose**

Isn't it funny how no one's ever allergic to chocolate biscuits.

Diet Tip
Yo-yo dieting doesn't work because Yo-Yos are chocolate biscuits and therefore not part of a calorie-controlled diet.

10 LIES A WOMAN TELLS HERSELF WHEN SHE CAN'T FACE THE FACT SHE MIGHT HAVE PUT ON WEIGHT:

'It must have shrunk in the wash.'

'They've put the wrong label in this skirt – the 14 is too tight and that's not right.'

*'Maybe I'm pregnant.'
(You're 62)*

'Well, I hardly eat a thing.'

'I must have some allergy that puffs me up.'

'I'm a martyr to water retention.'

'It's my metabolism.'

'Well, I have shot up recently.'

'I don't do kilos.'

'It's all muscle.'

DIET DO'S

1. Put your food on a very small plate.

2. Eat in your bikini in front of a mirror to remind yourself just how fat you really are.

3. Chew every mouthful 226 times, with any luck you'll only have time for one meal a day.

4. Wear a very tight belt and whatever you do, don't loosen it.

5. Get a friend to tie your hands behind your back or wear boxing gloves, you won't be able to open the cupboard door, never mind unwrap a Penguin bar.

6. Always use chopsticks. Eating a Mars bar with chopsticks is impossible – do not interpret this as a challenge.

7. Go to bed rather than sitting up with the biscuit tin and a bottle of pudding wine.

8. Hang out with your thin friends. The fat ones will sabotage your diet by slipping you toffees and ordering you a full-fat latte instead of a 'skinny' one out of spite.

Diary of a failed dieter

A **Wendy** *true-life* experience

Monday

6:30AM WOKE UP BRIGHT AND EARLY. REALLY EXCITED TO BE STARTING MY NEW HEALTH AND FITNESS REGIME. I'M FEELING REALLY POSITIVE THIS TIME AND RARING TO GO. DECIDED TO KICK START THE PROCEEDINGS WITH A QUICK JOG AROUND THE PARK, BUT UNFORTUNATELY I HAD A KNOT IN THE LACES OF MY TRAINERS AND WHEN I TRIED TO UNDO IT THE LACE BROKE. OH WELL, I ONCE READ AN ARTICLE BY THE MARATHON RUNNER PAULA RADCLIFFE WHERE SHE SAID THAT IT'S SILLY TO GO OUT RUNNING WITHOUT THE PROPER EQUIPMENT. SO I DID WHAT PAULA WOULD HAVE DONE AND WENT BACK TO BED.

8:30AM WOKE UP FOR THE SECOND TIME, SLIGHTLY LATER THAN ANTICIPATED. HAD HOPED TO COOK MYSELF A HEALTHY EGG-WHITE OMELETTE BEFORE SETTING OFF FOR WORK, BUT UNFORTUNATELY I SEEM TO HAVE FORGOTTEN TO BUY EGGS. DECIDED TO SKIP BREAKFAST AND PICKED UP A BLACK COFFEE ON MY WAY TO THE BUS STOP. THE GIRL SITTING NEXT TO ME ON THE 159 WAS EATING A MUFFIN AND SMILING AS SHE LICKED THE CRUMBS OFF HER LIPS. BITCH.

11AM FELT A LITTLE FAINT AND ATE A TANGERINE THAT HAS BEEN GOING OFF IN THE BOTTOM OF MY BAG FOR A COUPLE OF WEEKS. IT'S MARY IN THE OFFICE'S BIRTHDAY AND SHE BROUGHT IN SOME MERINGUES. NO ONE EVEN NOTICED WHEN I POLITELY DECLINED; MARY JUST SAID, 'WELL I'LL HAVE YOURS.' AND THEN BANGED ON ABOUT HAVING A 'REALLY FAST METABOLISM OR SOMETHING'. I SAID THE 'SOMETHING' MIGHT BE A TAPEWORM, BUT I DID IT UNDER MY BREATH AND SO NO ONE HEARD.

EVERYONE WENT OFF TO CELEBRATE MARY'S BIRTHDAY AT THE LOCAL PIZZA PLACE, BUT I STAYED BEHIND TO DO SOME EXTRA WORK. NO ONE OFFERED TO STAY AND HELP. I TRIED TO DO SOME PHOTOCOPYING BUT CAME OVER ALL DIZZY. APPARENTLY WHEN SUPERMODELS GET FAINT FROM HUNGER THEY EAT TISSUES. I CAN'T SAY IT WORKS FOR ME. CRACKED AND HAD A CEREAL BAR. A BIT OF IT FELL ON THE FLOOR AND EVEN THOUGH IT TOOK ME AGES TO FIND IT AND THE CARPET ISN'T THE CLEANEST, I ATE IT WHEN I FOUND IT. I ALSO ATE A SLIGHTLY FLUFFY MALTESER THAT I FOUND UNDER SONIA'S DESK.

5:30PM   HOME TIME AND NOT A MOMENT TOO SOON. ON THE BUS THERE WERE SOME TEENAGERS EATING CRISPS. THE SMELL OF SALT AND VINEGAR FILLED MY NOSTRILS AND MY BRAIN AND I GOT WORRIED THAT I MIGHT START SNATCHING, SO DECIDED TO GET OFF THE BUS, RATHER THAN CAUSE A SCENE.

SOMEHOW MANAGED TO MISJUDGE WHERE THE PAVEMENT WAS AND LANDED AWKWARDLY ON THE KERB TWISTING MY ANKLE VERY BADLY INDEED. I TRIED TO STAND UP, BUT MY ANKLE COULDN'T TAKE THE WEIGHT AND I COLLAPSED. WAS VERY UPSET AT THE PROSPECT OF NOT BEING ABLE TO GO TO BUMS AND TUMS TONIGHT AND IN A MOMENT OF SELF-PITY, DECIDED TO ORDER A TAKEAWAY PIZZA TO CHEER MYSELF UP.

WHEN I GOT HOME, I WAS IN AGONY. I MANAGED TO HOBBLE TO THE KITCHEN FOR A CAN OF LAGER AND AS I SAT ON THE SOFA, WAITING FOR THE PIZZA TO ARRIVE, MY ANKLE THROBBING GENTLY, I THOUGHT, 'OH WELL TOMORROW IS ANOTHER DAY.'

XX WENDY

EAT-ALL-YOU-WANT (CARDBOARD) DIET

We all lead busy lives, and let's face it, none of us have time to weigh out our food or count the calories on a daily basis. Here at *Wendy* we've been looking for a simple, easy to follow diet that leaves you feeling satisfied while giving you the results you need – and we think we've found it with this new Eat-All-You-Want Cardboard Diet. The beauty of this is that you don't need to cook something separate for you and the family; you can feed the family as normal and feast yourself on the wrapping. Economical as well as effective. Follow this step-by-step diet and we guarantee you will shed poundage.

Breakfast
Your metabolic rate is at its fastest during the first hour of the day, so feast yourself on as much cardboard as you like:
One cereal packet – family size – Special K or Sugar Puffs – yes, you truly can breakfast on Sugar Puffs (the box not the insides). One mug of hot water with a squeeze of lemon.

Elevenses
Two medium-size boxes e.g. a Cup a Soup box or a basmati rice box, with a dash of Worcester sauce if desired.

Lunch
Egg box terrine. Simply whiz an egg box in the liquidiser with some tap water, season and heat on high in a microwave for two and a half minutes, stirring at one minute and leaving to rest for five minutes.

Supper
Polystyrene meat tray (not family pack).
Side dish of kitchen roll.
Jaffa cake (packet) for those of you that have a sweet tooth.

Weekend treat
Fruit polystyrene holder for pears.
Cheese cracker box (medium size) – surprisingly filling.

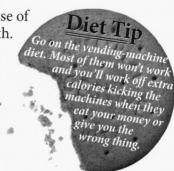
Diet Tip
Go on the vending-machine diet. Most of them won't work and you'll work off extra calories kicking the machines when they eat your money or give you the wrong thing.

YULE LOVE OUR
FESTIVE IDEAS

Customise some cardboard for Christmas with this Festive cardboard log – diets need not be dull!

Empty the contents out of two washing powder boxes (medium), one packet of dried lentils and two nectarine trays, simmer in water for two hours, stirring occasionally.

Discard the paper contents of two kitchen rolls, and use the cardboard holders as a mould around which to drape your mixture. Leave to set in the fridge. Garnish with cotton wool snowmen.

Serving suggestion

If you liked that why not try a real log, only 22 calories per bite!

Diet Tip

Only eat free food – like the free things they put on the deli counter at Waitrose – after a while they'll see you coming and pretend they've run out.

Why not start now? Savour the subtle inky flavour of this delicious paper. Garnish with black pepper or if you're feeling adventurous a pinch of nutmeg.

TASTY

Philip Glenister

DIET DON'TS

1 Drink alcohol.

2 Kid yourself that carrot cake is OK. Just because it's got the word 'carrot' in it doesn't mean it's slimming; neither will it help you see in the dark.

3 Eat your children's leftover pizza crusts.

4 Lick the lid of a carton of cream.

5 Pretend that you only had one crisp. You didn't, you had seven.

6 Accidentally shovel a Twix into your mouth.

7 Eat stale cake that you are pretending to, put out for the birds.

8 Offer to do the washing up and tidy the kitchen just so that you can gorge yourself on leftovers.

9 Check your children's lunch boxes for bits of uneaten sandwiches.

10 Eat those little freebie morsels of cheese and pork pie that they are offering down at the supermarket.

11 Opt for the all-you-can-eat £3.99 Chinese lunch buffets.

12 Spoon jam straight into your mouth from the jar.

Fashion Ideas for the Beach

Beaches are perilous places for the over-forties. Look good in a bikini and the other middle-aged women will despise you; if you're averagely plump to very plump, all the other women will spend their time asking their partners/friends/children whether they look as fat as you do. Congratulations, you have become the beach **FAT-O-METER**.

Lying flat on the sunbed is one solution, since most people look (marginally) slimmer lying down. It also has the added bonus of making it impossible to eat or drink, which in the long run is a good idea.

DO

1 As Coco Chanel might once have said, 'Accessorise, accessorise, accessorise', and when you think you've done enough accessorising, accessorise some more!

2 Wear big straw hats and big sunglasses. The bigger the hat, the smaller the hips will look by comparison.

3 Read an interesting book. At least people will think you're a fat intellectual.

4 If you can bear it, wear a high heeled wedge, tricky on the beach but worth persevering with. Perhaps you could practise in the winter months in a kiddie's sandpit. Basically, fat that is four inches off the ground looks better than flattie fat!

5 Invest in a sensible towel, lying on a George from Asda screams budget; draping yourself across a Gucci or Prada number screams more money than sense. What you want is something bright and cheerful, maybe even stripy, from John Lewis. A little tip is to carry it over your arm waiter-style to cover a flabby tummy.

6 Carry a large beach bag at all times to cover unsightly flab (also useful for carrying around everyone else's rubbish, as well as the stuff you nicked from the breakfast buffet. Job done).

DON'T

1 Be tempted to go in for the Joan Collins St. Tropez look, i.e. leopard skin sarong, flip flops with rhinestone detail, large sunglasses, bright red nails, and full make-up. To pull this off you have to be on first name terms with your cosmetic surgeon, very wealthy, and be in denial about your real age.

2 Think your bra and pants can pass as swim wear. Once they've had a good soaking you will see the error of your ways, as will everyone else.

3 Play ball games – people will flee for fear of bosoms bouncing out of captivity.

4 Let anyone take any photos of you unless you are treading water out of your depth in the sea (and looking up).

5 Get hysterical if you fall through a deckchair. You will only draw attention to yourself.

6 Over coordinate. Yes, they sell cossies, sarongs, beach bags, and hats to match in that riot of turquoise and yellow parrot print, but it doesn't mean you should buy all four together. You'll just look like you've got busy with some old, loose covers.

Tips for looking good in the Sun

We all love the summer, long hot days and evenings spent sitting out in the garden, drinking Pimms. But as we all know, for every silver lining there must be a cloud. With summer, it's taking off your thick, comforting, woolly, opaque tights and exposing your bare legs, and more, to the world.

Oh, how much easier it would have been to look good in the sun back in those days when photos were in black and white and people were taken down to the water's edge in a beach hut on wheels and slipped surreptitiously into the water wearing a stripy baby grow for grown-ups.

One option might be to spend your hols on the Russian Riviera because all the other women tend to be old boilers who have spent a lifetime making cheap dumplings and eating them. Hoorah! You will be the Belle of the beach. On the other hand, you could book a couple of weeks in the Lake District or Wales, somewhere it's guaranteed to rain constantly so you won't even have to unpack your cozzie. Instead, you can sit on the beach in your anorak eating flapjacks and drinking hot soup out of a thermos flask. Bliss.

fake tan

1 Buy the best you can afford and wash your hands after. Those bright orange palms are such a giveaway.

avoid khaki shorts

2 If you've got a big bottom, don't wear massive khaki shorts, you will look like a cross between Captain Mainwairing and a very bossy lesbian. Go for a nice, floaty skirt and a loose top instead.

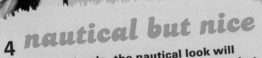

avoid nylon

3 You will sweat like a pig, especially if you are carrying excess weight.

nautical but nice

4 Keep it simple, the nautical look will give the impression that you know what you're doing stylistically, even if you haven't really got a clue. Just remember 'navy and white, just right'. However don't be tempted to go overboard – a sailor's hat is a step too far!

If all else fails, take lessons from those short, fat, Greek women. They've got the right idea: swathe yourself in black cotton and buy yourself a donkey.

avoid red...

5 Avoid wearing the colour red if you have a pale complexion and burn in the sun. It will call attention to the shocking colour contrast and you'll end up looking like a barber's pole.

THE SARONG'S

What on earth did we do before sarongs? They are quite simply God's gift to women everywhere – covering up flabby bits, crinkly bits, blotchy bits and bullet wounds. But here's the added bonus, think how useful they are for other things…

- For waving down the helicopter or emergency services.
- For tying round your jaw in a double knot to stop you eating those Kettle Chips on the happy hour bar.
- For putting shampoo and shower cap freebies in as you pass the chambermaid trolley in the corridor.
- And most importantly for bagsying sun loungers, chairs, best tables in the restaurant, and generally staking claim to things you feel are rightfully yours.

If you are going away for a week, take a fresh sarong for every day and accessorise with different jewellery and flip flops.

However, you will need to study the sarong knots opposite to avoid looking like someone who has just had a temporary sling put on by the St Johns ambulance.

DICK WHITTINGTON STYLE
For the greedy cost conscious mum – ideal for sneaking stolen breakfast buffet items down to the beach.

THE SOLUTION

OFF THE SHOULDER
A statement rather than the purely functional.

ROUND THE HIPS
For the pear-shaped lady who has a great top half to show off.

THE HALTER NECK
For those with a hot figure but a problematic creasy neck and cleavage. Not in any circumstances to be worn by people with bingo wings.

WHAT YOUR FAVOURITE PUDDING SAYS ABOUT YOU AND YOUR LOVE LIFE

POISON IVAN TURNS HIS CROOKED HAND TO GASTRONOMY TO REVEAL THE AMOROUS TRUTHS BEHIND YOUR CHOICE OF DESSERT.

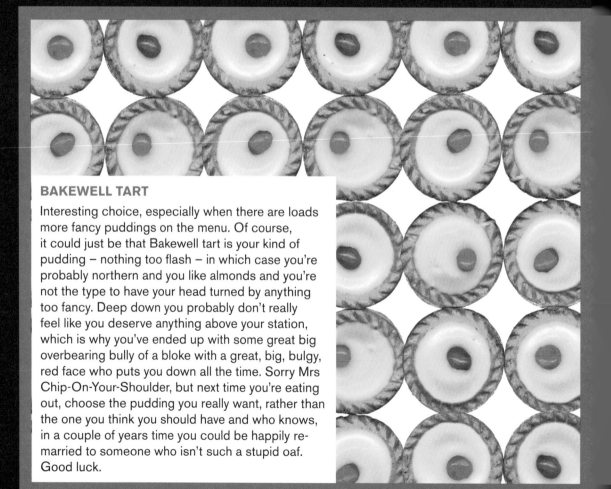

BAKEWELL TART

Interesting choice, especially when there are loads more fancy puddings on the menu. Of course, it could just be that Bakewell tart is your kind of pudding – nothing too flash – in which case you're probably northern and you like almonds and you're not the type to have your head turned by anything too fancy. Deep down you probably don't really feel like you deserve anything above your station, which is why you've ended up with some great big overbearing bully of a bloke with a great, big, bulgy, red face who puts you down all the time. Sorry Mrs Chip-On-Your-Shoulder, but next time you're eating out, choose the pudding you really want, rather than the one you think you should have and who knows, in a couple of years time you could be happily re-married to someone who isn't such a stupid oaf. Good luck.

VANILLA ICE CREAM

How old are you? Ice cream is for children and people recovering from tonsillectomies, it's hardy the choice of a sophisticated woman of the world.

Where's your sense of adventure? You probably like teddies on the bed and talk in a baby voice now and again, which some strange men quite like but which gravely offends most normal women. Your problem is that you're scared of trying something new and will always go for the safe option. Essentially, you're a coward, which is why you have ended up in a safe but rather dull marriage with a tedious sex life. Why not try something new? You might not like it, but as long as it doesn't hurt and it's legal, it might just get you out of that rut.

TRIFLE

Who's a greedy Miss Piggy? You are! You're the woman who wants the lot: excitement, surprises, sponge fingers, cold custard, cooking sherry and lashings of whipped cream. You're a good-time girl but a little bit lazy to boot, and life for you is best when it's spoon fed with a cherry on top. You're a natural born flirt and doubtless prefer the company of men to women, but you're also greedy and selfish so you'd choose money over love any day. Watch yourself missy, you're not getting any younger but you are getting more thread veins. Get a grip, lady.

GOOSEBERRY FOOL

Frankly sweetheart, you are a bit mad. No one in their right mind likes gooseberries more than anything else. You want to stand out from the crowd but this will often backfire and end up with you making an idiot of yourself. Most of the time you are in a state of regret because you have made another daft choice, be it buying the wrong car or having sex with the wrong man or having sex with the right man in the wrong place, which is why you've ended up in court… again.

★ WENDY CHEATS RECIPES

Now that even Delia Smith has turned into a lazy convenience food slut, us hard-working certain-agers can admit to cutting culinary corners. Here are some nutritious and delicious recipes that combine the best of fresh ingredients with some really SLAP DASH kitchen habits:

#1 Meringue Bombe

★Buy two of those packs of MERINGUE NEST things

★Bung them in a plastic bag and knot the end. Grab a rolling pin and beat the hell out of the bag (Not literally because it will burst and then your kitchen will be full of meringue dust and look like it did when those tilers were in last year)

★Chuck the lumps of meringue in a bowl

★Put a large tub of double cream in that you've whipped (or bought whipped)

★Chuck some brandy in or something alcoholic if you haven't already drunk it

★Put it in a round basin in the freezer and cover with some foil or a plate

★Lick the bowl before anyone else gets it

When your mother-in-law comes round, bring your basin out, stand it in a washing up bowl of hot water for a second or two to loosen the edges, then dollop on a plate, round-side-up, and put a load of strawberries or such around the edge. Voila, domestic goddess.

#2 TRIFLE

Buy a pack of trifle sponges
Bung half of them in the bottom of a glass dish and throw some sherry on top Melt some red jam in a saucepan and pour a bit on – especially satisfying since it feels like using up leftovers, so don't buy a jar
Chuck a tin of some sort of drained fruit in, and chop, say, a peach, a kiwi or two pears and a banana (not an apple, they go brown) into the dish
Put a layer of instant custard on that has cooled a bit, and a layer of double cream
Grate some chocolate on the top and eat the rest of the bar yourself.

TRIFLE

#3 Idiot-proof chicken risotto

For four:
- Two tubs of new Covent Garden mushroom risotto
- Half a bottle red wine or white, depending on what you've got left
- Some fancy mushrooms or normal ones if you don't want to fork out for fancy
- Some leftover olives that have been hanging around in the fridge
- Frozen peas (a tsp each)
- A ready-cooked chicken

Cook the mushrooms in tiny amount of olive oil in largish pan. Add tubs of risotto, shred and add chicken – no bones obviously. Put on low heat, add half bottle of red (or white) wine and the peas and olives, stir now and again for about ten minutes. Serve with <u>plenty of parmesan</u> and maybe some spinach if you've got some.

#4 Chicken and mushroom pie

Fry some chicken breasts in butter, chop them up a bit with a pair of scissors into a heavy saucepan or something, chuck in some mushrooms and fry them a bit, then a tin of chicken soup. Cook for about 15 minutes or until you get very impatient and bored.
Roll out some flaky pastry that comes in a packet.
Bung the chicken in the bottom of a pie dish, put a slice of pastry on the top and then score the top with a cross like your mother used to do when she implied it had taken her three hours. Put in the oven until pastry is brown.

#5 Easy peasy tomato sauce

- Cut tomatoes in half
- Put on oven dish which you have chucked a load of olive oil on
- Chop up a clove or two of garlic
- Whip in some basil leaves
- Sprinkle in some salt and pepper
- Bake for 25 minutes or so
- Liquidise

Peel and chop a couple of largish potatoes

Chop an onion or some spring onions, depending on wrist strength

Throw them both in thick-based pan with some butter or some dripping that you've saved in little mugs in the back of the fridge

Swirl about a bit while you call the plumber (again) or check whether teenagers are doing homework, but don't leave it too long as it will burn and make you bad tempered

Throw in a packet of watercress, ideally washed

Stir it about and put the lid on for a few minutes to let it sweat

Put the kettle on and pour about a pint of hot water on a chicken stock cube, or if you are a veggie, then veggie stock cube

Simmer with lid on for about 20 minutes until potatoes are done

Meanwhile go off and do some little jobs, or better yet, go and check whether someone else has done the little jobs you gave them to do earlier

Text a friend

Put it all in the whizzer

Serve with a bit of fresh cream and a dash of nutmeg and salt and pepper and make it look like you have slaved over the stove for hours

#7 Hugely Fattening but Delicious Garlic Potatoes

Get someone to peel about six large potatoes

Butter one of those oblong oven dishes

Slice the potatoes as thinly as you can be bothered

Between each layer of potatoes put some big dollops of butter, some even bigger dollops of double cream and salt, pepper and some garlic

Build up the layers and then finish with more cream and butter and cheese, if you're feeling especially greedy, on the top

Put in a hot oven for about 40 minutes or until golden brown

Serves 4 greedy people

#8 Phenomenal Pesto Sauce

Get the liquidiser out of that annoying cupboard with everything stacked on top of everything else and with that stupid popcorn maker that you never use

*6 tablespoons of <u>decent</u> olive oil

*A garlic clove

*A pack of pine nuts

*Grate some parmesan cheese — about a cup full or if you can't be bothered to (even) do that chuck in a packet of grated stuff

*One of those packs of basil leaves or if you have a plant of the stuff on the kitchen window sill tear the leaves off it and leave it looking like it has been napalmed

<u>Whiz</u>↓

#9 Souper Beany Supper

1 carton of Covent Garden vegetable soup, or
chilli bean, or any tin or packet of veg soup
1 tin of baked beans, any brand
Slosh together in a saucepan and stir until hot,
but not so hot it's going to take the skin off the
roof of your mouth
Add a splash of Worcestershire sauce and
parmesan and, hey presto, a hearty supper that's
suitable for any vegetarian who might happen
to pop by

WHAT YOUR CHOICE OF TEA TOWEL SAYS ABOUT YOU AND YOUR COOKING

POISON IVAN, OUR VERY OWN FASCIST FASHIONISTA, WIPES THE FLOOR WITH YOUR CHOICE OF OVEN DRAPE.

TRADITIONAL WHITE WITH RED BORDER – CAFÉ STYLE

You're a lady who says a big fat NO to novelty, a stickler for the real deal, and why shouldn't you be? These tea towels are kitchen classics and you're a girl who knows her way around a Fish kettle. You've got a black belt in pastry making: choux, short crust or flaky, you name it, you can put it in a bowl, mash it up with your great big bare fists and shove it in the oven without breaking into a sweat. You're probably quite a big girl, a no-nonsense, kitchen Brunhilda, with all the pans, knives, filthy temper and possible alcohol problem that goes hand in hand with being a good cook.

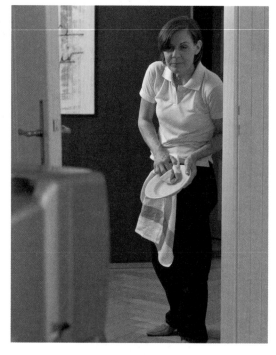

MOST LIKELY TO COOK: BOEUF EN CROUTE OR JUGGED HARE STEEPED IN IT'S OWN BLOOD.

PENGUIN
BOOKS

MYSTERY & CRIME

THE LABOU
OF HERCU

AGATHA CHRI

COMPLETE   UN

TEA TOWEL WITH PENGUIN CLASSIC AGATHA CHRISTIE BOOK COVER DESIGN

Aren't we the smug one? I bet you buy loads of home décor mags and get a bit squealy with excitement when you've already got something in your house that's featured in this month's *Elle Deco*. Like many style sheep, you think you're more original than you actually are and get incredibly stressed out trying to find the right shaped potato peeler. You're the type of woman who can easily spend forty quid on a colander, but who can't really cook. Thank God for Marks, eh? Basic domestic science is something you didn't really do at school because you were one of the clever ones doing extra Latin, so now you've got the kitchen skills of an eleven-year-old and even though you're yet to master gravy, you've booked yourself into a roll your own sushi workshop for your dinner party. Thing is, most of your friends think you're a pretentious twat.

MOST LIKELY TO COOK: *A SALAD WITH SOMETHING FASHIONABLE IN IT, LIKE POMEGRANATE.*

Willow Park Primary School

PAUL

SIMON

Anna.R.

KEVIN

BRIAN

EMMa

Rebecca

Thelma

WiLi

TiM

MATT

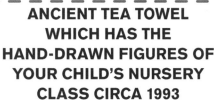

ANCIENT TEA TOWEL WHICH HAS THE HAND-DRAWN FIGURES OF YOUR CHILD'S NURSERY CLASS CIRCA 1993

No prizes for guessing what you are. That's right, a sentimental old fool! Every time you use this tea towel you remember when your little boy Tim was in the red class at nursery and you were a bit worried about his co-ordination because his was the worst self portrait on the tea towel.

You're a terrible old hoarder and have bits of greaseproof paper in one of those rickety old drawers that have been lining pastry cases for over a decade. You are a good cook but slightly forgetful and sometimes you find yourself wandering down the high street in your nightie with your wooden spoon. All your kitchen utensils are ancient and battered and the plastic ones have all got melted twisted ends. You keep your biscuits in a Charles and Diana (such a shame) tin and your oven gloves are a certifiable health hazard.

MOST LIKELY TO COOK: ENOUGH LASAGNE FOR TEN, EVEN THOUGH YOU LIVE ON YOUR OWN.

NATIONAL TRUST TEA TOWEL

You're not fussed in the slightest what's on your tea towel. As far as you're concerned, a tea towel is for wiping things, be it plates, muddy footprints or dog sick. People who are fussy about tea towels are silly ninnies and you are most certainly not one of those. In fact, you haven't cried since you were seven when a combine harvester took off your arm. You like a bit of wildlife, and can identify different trees and birds and ninnies, but even though you're a nature lover you don't get squeamish when the cat drops a dead bird at your feet – you just pop it down the waste disposal and get on with your day. Cooking is something you can either take or leave, even if you are surprisingly good at things like crème caramel and decorative icing (with your one good arm).

MOST LIKELY TO COOK: A PICNIC. THERE'S NO WAY YOU'RE GOING TO PAY SILLY PRICES WHEN YOU CAN SIT IN THE CAR WITH A FLASK OF HOT SOUP AND A HARD BOILED EGG.

Wendy's Short Stories

OLD FLAMES

Everyone seemed to be going on about school reunions, looking up old school pals on Friends Reunited or Facebook, but Christine had avoided it uptil now. Avoided it not (just) because she was busy, but because she knew that if she saw his photo there, on the website, looking twenty-five years older it would disturb her – either because he looked just the same, or because he looked entirely different; either way it would be hard, because deep down she knew she never really stopped loving Ian, not really.

It wasn't that she was unhappy with her life as it had become. Richard was a good father and a good husband, 'a good man', as people always said. He had been supportive when she had wanted to retrain as a podiatrist, had helped her with the kids when they were little – changed more than his fair share of nappies, had done his share of the night shift when they were babies, even though his job was so much more important than hers. They had a lot in common and rubbed along pretty well, getting on with the things people get on with endlessly in daily life.

Richard insisted on them going out once a fortnight on a Saturday night, thought it was important to take some time out together. He even made a bit of an effort to look good, and to take her new places once in a while. But the truth is they had little to say to one another. Christine remembered how she had looked at couples like them when she was young, perhaps on holiday, empty nesters like them with little or nothing left to say to one another, looking like they might be a bit desperate to strike up conversation, or a bit clingy if you got pally with them, couples not exactly unhappy but where the fire had obviously gone out. Sometimes, after they had been out for their ritual meal, they ended up making love, but often it would take Richard a good half an hour to come up to bed once they got home, doing a sudoku or tidying some papers up. Their marriage wasn't exactly passionate, and although Richard knew what she liked, or what she told him she liked all those years ago, it didn't feel like anything very spontaneous was ever going to happen again.

She'd avoided Ian or the prospect of Ian for all these years, but one day she found herself googling

'Needless to say the googling didn't find him...'

his name. Ian MacIntyre was clearly a common name from Sidcup to Sydney and back again, and she didn't imagine for a minute that he was either the serial killer on death row in Colorado or the celebrity chef in New Zealand. What an amazing thing the internet is, she thought. It started her wondering, wondering what had happened to him and thinking that really she should be grown up enough to be able to find out what he was doing, where he lived, how many kids he had – and not rock the boat. Needless to say the googling didn't find him, and the truth was she wasn't sure she wanted to find him anyway.

The Christmas round robin from Donna arrived as usual, longer and duller than usual, which was saying something. Donna took keeping in touch with friends very seriously, so seriously that she continued to send Christine her annual news with shocking regularity and attention to detail. Donna lived in Colorado, which is why she took keeping in touch with her past so seriously. Donna would know – if anyone would know – what had become of Ian.

Donna was pleasantly surprised to hear from Christine Holmes (as she was then). Excited at the unexpected flurry of emails, she sent Donna some old netball team photos that she fished out from somewhere – which thrilled the hell out of Donna. Christine knew that sooner or later she would send her a group email of the others, the others from the class of '79, and so eventually she did. And there was Ian's name and email address.

Christine did nothing for a week, reasoned that if she still thought it was a good idea in a few days' time she would send a chatty, cheery email and then she could at least say to herself she'd tried. After a week it seemed like a bad idea, but she emailed anyway, a group email seemed safest – and she could wait to see whether Ian would find her email address and email back, whether she would trigger his radar, like the concept of him triggered hers. She waited and Trish and Don and Jean and Carol all replied with affectionate catch-ups, but nothing from Ian.

'...she hadn't even put her nice frilly underwear on...'

All of a sudden the email came. She had given him up, felt not a small amount of relief that Ian either was indifferent to her, or was off the radar for good, but Ian emailed her direct, not even the newsy round robin that she had disguised hers with, but one sent just to her.

It was the smell and the taste of him that was so shockingly familiar. After nearly twenty-five years, they kissed, and it seemed like the most natural thing in the world, the easiest kiss ever, not even very sexy but a genuine kiss, a kiss that made her feel alive, excited, wanted, loved, looked at, special, in a way that she realised Richard had never made her feel. It was as if Ian knew her inside out, knew the person she really was. They made love, something that Christine didn't imagine would happen – she hadn't even put her nice frilly underwear on, nor even thought about condoms – she should have realised. I suppose, she thought, this is what grown ups do when they get passionate.

It wasn't like they were eighteen again, she reasoned, and a little bit hesitant or that they had their whole lives before them to decide whether they should or they shouldn't.

Ian certainly seemed as if he thought it was what their meeting would lead to – there was a certain assumption, in his hotel room. It was eleven in the morning. Ian had obviously done whatever people have to do to get a room for the day, which presumably is code for some illegitimate nooky. Christine could hear the maid hoovering outside in the corridor, it all felt odd, a bit cheap, a bit empty. Passionate, yes, on his part; sexy, yes, but once the kissing stopped and the sex started it felt like a mistake. She felt like calling a halt to it, to say 'Look, can we just get back to the kissing', but it was too late – Ian was well away.

She didn't like the way he pushed her head down, assumed that she would give him a blow-job. Richard had never done that, never forced her to do anything she didn't want to, and when Christine stopped, went to the bathroom and got dressed, Ian looked angry.

'What do you think you're doing?' he said.

'I'm saying goodbye to my adolescence,' she said, and she gathered her things and walked out without looking back to take a last look at him.

Christine realised that her life with Richard was agreeable, safe, comfortable, and loving – not in a passionate way, but in the ways that matter, with a family together and a joint history and journey that could not be replaced by a man with more testosterone than is good for a man of fifty-two and a liking for recreational sex. She was too old for recreational sex, and she was glad about it.

THE END

Invisibilty – How to avoid it!

'It's a well-known fact that after a certain age women tend to blend in with the background and become, to all intents and purposes, invisible'. DR. RUDOLF CLERC

 In fact, in his seminal paper, *Woman, Where Have You Gone?*, the German psychiatrist Wilfred Kestler cited an example of a woman who was squashed to death by her husband who sat on her because he didn't realise she was there.

Modern opinion tends to the view that whilst women cannot literally disappear into the ether, the older and uglier a woman becomes, the less likely younger, more attractive people are to notice her.

Symptoms include:

- Not getting served in the pub.
- Waiters forgetting your meal so you get your first course when everyone else is eating their pudding.
- Being left behind at a motorway service station by your coach party.
- Work colleagues bitching about you, even though you are sitting right next to them.
- Your next-door neighbour of four years asking if you are 'new to these parts'?
- Having to witness a couple having sex on the bus because they thought they were alone.
- Being left in a changing room in your bra and pants by an assistant who was meant to be getting you a size 16 and just forgot you were there.

How to avoid the invisibility syndrome

- Make a big noisy fuss.
- Shout at the top of your voice. The posher you sound the more attention you will receive.
- Wear a see-through top and no bra.
- Hang out with your famous mate. If you haven't got one, dress up a friend to look like Joan Collins (young gay men are quite good at pulling this one off).
- Pretend you are breast feeding/pregnant.
- Use your umbrella to poke people who are not paying you enough attention.

- Have something strange on a lead, like a rabbit or a lizard.
- Skip. People are quite scared of anyone over the age of ten skipping.
- Make eye contact with men over fifty who haven't had a woman look at them in decades – the balder and uglier the better. Look at them and wink; your invisibility will disappear instantly and you will make a whole heap of neglected middle-aged men feel loads better.

If however you are still invisible,
why not embrace your invisibility?
If people really can't see you,
think what fun you can have
helping yourself to blueberry
muffins at Starbucks!

10 ways to...

make him notice you!

1
Pretend to be on your mobile phone and laugh. It will make him think you have friend(s) and a sense of humour.

3
Pretend to have cramp in the deep end. If he attempts to rescue you, or at least alerts the life guard you're in with a chance.

2
Bandage up your wrist. If he's got any manners he'll ask you what happened. Tell him that you fell off some decking at Jane Asher's house – he will be intrigued that you know a cake-baking celebrity.

4
Read a book in a foreign language. He will assume you are bilingual and be intrigued by your cleverness.

5
Look really sad. He might offer to buy you a drink to cheer you up. Don't let him 'cheer' you up so much that you end up under the table trying to find your tights.

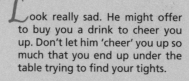

6

Cover your hands in engine oil. He will wonder what such a feminine 'girl' such as yourself is doing with 'mechanic's hands'. Say you were changing the carburettor on your classic MG, and he might just start salivating.

9

Drop 'When I was at the National' into conversation. He will presume you were on stage, not selling ice creams in the interval. Learn a few lines from *Romeo and Juliet* which you can mutter mysteriously and theatrically under your breath.

7

Wear stockings. Simple but effective (as long as they're on your legs and not on your head).

10

Avoid him. Stay away from the pub/ park/ salsa class, all those places where you usually bump into him. He will either pine for you and be really pleased to see you when you next decide to show up, or completely forget your name and start dating that Scandinavian tart who can tango like an Argentinean prostitute.

8

Do a cartwheel. Practise first otherwise it could end in tears.

PULLING OUTFITS
FOR THE MATURE WOMAN

One of the big advantages of being a woman of a certain age is that we don't have to go out clubbing with other women on a Saturday night and totter around on heels hoping to be chatted up – either we are stopping in with our partners having an argument or sitting at home stroking our cat. However, sometimes we find ourselves unavoidably divorced or in need of some male company, especially if we have stroked our cats bald, in which case there is nothing else for it but to find a pulling outfit that works.

Choosing a pulling outfit when you are, let's say, over thirty-five is a challenging business. You used to be able to wear a short skirt or a sleeveless dress with a plunging neckline and you would look like a million dollars. Now you end up looking like Judy Finnegan in Paris Hilton's clothes, or like a slightly younger version of Barbara Windsor.

You want to send out the slightly available message, without looking desperate. And here's how:

Let's start with the shoes. Don't go beyond the kitten heel, anything bigger than a medium spike will turn you instantly into Dick Emery. Also, you don't know who you might fancy; it could be that short fat millionaire and you don't want to be towering over him, so ideally you want to keep yourself under five foot six. Do not go for the open toe, unless you have compared your toes with all of your friends' toes and they have been pronounced normal. If your toes are crossed and the nails are the colour of walnuts, keep them hidden – they are your terrible secret. Yours alone.

However good your legs are, don't be tempted to go for a very short skirt. His mother will be in her eighties and won't approve. OK, so what you wear has got nothing to do with his mother, but there's no need to start those kind of arguments before you've even met. Play safe: your skirt should touch the knee and ride up slightly when you cross your legs, making a slightly raspy noise as the nylon slides against the silk of your underskirt. Men are like dogs, their ears tune into these kinds of noises and they start panting.

The rule of cleavage is simple, expose a tiny bit more with every date. Obviously, you can only do this up to a point – never go to the extent of getting them out over a pub lunch. At least wait until you get back in the car.

Walking the dog is a great place to pull as you get older – so dump that smelly old anorak and get yourself some attention-seeking wellies or jazzy jumpers for those lovely autumnal mornings when he might be walking out his mutt too.

Once you have dolled yourself up in a healthy outdoorsy way, make sure your pooch doesn't let you down. If you're dragging around a barely continent old lab with cataracts, swap it for a nice little puppy. No one can resist a puppy!

TIP
Do scoop that poop but don't attempt to chat him up whilst holding a plastic bag of doggy poo.

PS
Of course, the sad truth is that the best place to pull at our age is at a funeral: flattering black dress, shiny patent heels, and some nice sheer black tights – you're laughing. Well, OK, not laughing, but next time you are asked to a funeral keep your eyes skinned.

Good luck

Go for an open toe but only if your feet have been pronounced normal!

A skirt that touches the knee is just the ticket. Anything too short and you will look desperate

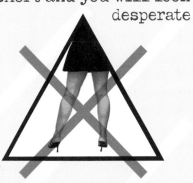

A little bit of cleavage might just catch his eye

Result!!

WHEN JEAN MET BARRY...

Jean and her friend are very excited...

JEAN, I CAN'T BELIEVE WE'VE GOT TICKETS TO SEE STEVE McDEE, I'D LOVE TO MEET HIM!

STEVE McDEE

STEVE'S SO FANTASTIC. I'D LOVE TO MEET HIM...

On the day of the concert, Jean is too excited to eat...

I'LL EAT LATER...

SEATS 1-20

THERE YOU GO, JEAN. A LARGE RED WINE TO GET YOU IN THE MOOD...

STEVE McDEE

Jean and her friends spend ages getting ready...

OH MAUREEN, THAT DRESS LOOKS GREAT ON YOU!

THANKS JEAN, YOU LOOK FAB TOO!

Suddenly over the tannoy...

PLEASE TAKE YOUR SEATS, TONIGHT'S CONCERT IS ABOUT TO BEGIN!!

Middle-Aged

DATING GAME

How To Play

Move forward and back on the squares of love, simply throw the dice and play our

dating game of chance and sod's law. Please provide your own dice

Finish

BACK TO START

Just when you think you've made it, you see his photofit on *Crimewatch*.

48

BACK 4

He says you're the most beautiful woman he's ever seen but he's diagnosed with cataracts.

36

BACK 3

...but lets you pay, even though you didn't mean it when you offered.

46

39

BACK 5

... and suggests a threesome.

FORWARD 4

He takes you out for a swish meal...

44

FORWARD 4

He wants to take you away for a weekend...

42 **41**

BACK 5
He wolf whistles when he sees you.

22

23

34

FORWARD 2
Hoorah you've lost three pounds.

8

7

20

FORWARD 3
He invites you round for dinner and makes a really good fish pie.

9

6

BACK 7
He says 'Shift it, grandma'.

21

19

10

5

BACK 8
You eat six hot cross buns without bothering to toast them.

18

FORWARD 5
He holds a door open for you.

31

32

FORWARD 8
He gives you his spare two-for-the-price-of-one packet of hot cross buns.

17

11

BACK 3
He pops round when you've been squeezing a massive spot on your chin.

29

26

START AGAIN
He likes your shoes. Hoorah, he noticed. Oh, oh, he's gay.

12

3

BACK 3
You fall over his walking stick.

28

30

FORWARD 2
He buys you flowers.

15

16

BACK 8
Something must have been off in that fish pie you suffer vomiting and diarrhoea.

13

2

Start

WEEKEND WARDROBE
to colour in

A chunky jumper for lovely brisk walks, nice and baggy so you can eat a massive pub lunch without worrying

T-shirt: choose colours that match your favourite ice cream flavours, that way you've more chance of stains not showing

A pleated sensible skirt for days when you want to be a 'stroppy old cow'

A pretty skirt for those days when you want to feel 'girlish'

A pair of trousers or jeans NB don't spoil your weekend by wearing the ones that look really good but are too tight – life is too short for uncomfortable trousers

What all of us want – a simple yet flexible weekend capsule wardrobe. There isn't a woman in the world who hasn't stood naked in front of her bulging wardrobe uttering the words **'I've got nothing to wear'.**

Obviously, this is a lie, you've got loads of clothes, but you hate them all: some are too small, some have gone baggy in the wash, some scream so last century, and some you bought after you'd been drinking at lunch time.

Our fashion gurus at **Wendy** are here to guide you through your wardrobe 'must have's – a few simple items that will take you from the farmers market to a trip to the bottle bank and an incalculably dull dinner party with the people over the road who are retired and talk about tracing their family tree till 11.30pm.

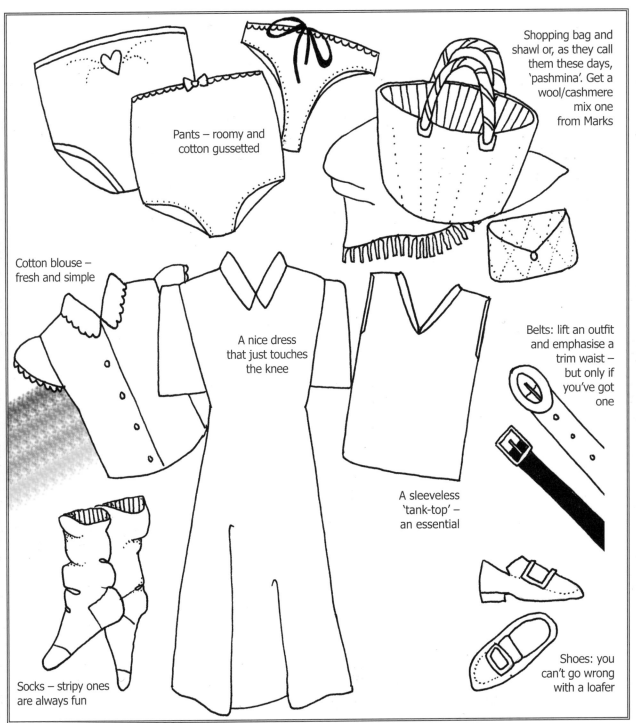

Pants – roomy and cotton gussetted

Shopping bag and shawl or, as they call them these days, 'pashmina'. Get a wool/cashmere mix one from Marks

Cotton blouse – fresh and simple

A nice dress that just touches the knee

Belts: lift an outfit and emphasise a trim waist – but only if you've got one

A sleeveless 'tank-top' – an essential

Socks – stripy ones are always fun

Shoes: you can't go wrong with a loafer

WHAT EVERY WOMAN NEEDS..

A TUNIC!

WHY EVERY WOMAN NEEDS A TUNIC!

The classic suits-every-size tunic never goes out of fashion. This easy-to-wear, elegant shift shape can be worn to the office or dolled up for a date!

Many of us get dressed in the morning without a clue where we're going to end up later on in the evening (probably back at home in front of the telly, but you never know). That's why it's important to have clothes that are socially versatile. And you can't get more versatile than the tunic!

FOUR WAYS OF WEARING A TUNIC:

A) With a jumper underneath

For chilly days – layer your tunic with a fine knit roll neck jersey underneath. Remember this year's fashionable colours include aubergine and lime.

B) With a blouse underneath

Blouses are such a good idea, especially if you get a bit hot and flustered in a woolly. All sorts of blouses look smashing under a tunic, choose between stripes, florals or even a paisley.

C) With a vibrant cardi

The vibrant cardi is ideal for the tunic wearer who can not control the temperature of her working environment. It's as easy to take off as it is to put on.

D) With an assortment of belts and scarves

We all know it's easy to transform an outfit with the clever use of accessories. In fact there are university courses now whereby you can gain a degree in accessorising – if you're not a talented accessoriser, why not look one up on the internet?

A

B

D

C

JEWELLERY

Chunky ethnic jewellery can really add that wow factor to the simple tunic, it will also act as a conversational opening gambit, which can be just the ticket at a slightly awkward drinks function.

Pearls are always classy and no one can really tell whether they're real or not, not unless they bite them.

SLEEPLESS

SLEEPLESS
NIGHTS

*W*e've all tussled with those sleepless nights, sighing and huffing through the night, watching as the hands on the alarm clock move inexorably through the small hours of the morning, creeping minute-by-minute closer to the time when you should be bouncing out of bed having had a good eight hours' kip. So why can't you sleep? Why are you lying there in the bed like a cross between a thrashing goldfish and a coiled spring? Well, let's think...

FIRST OF ALL LET'S CHECK ANY PRACTICAL ISSUES:

✳ Are you too cold? Check he's not hogging the duvet, or that your bare bottom isn't sticking out of your nightie into the cold night air.

✳ Are you too hot? In which case open a window, but only one that a burglar can't get through.

✳ Are you thirsty? Have a drink of water.

✳ Is he snoring? Wear ear plugs.

OK, if none of those are keeping you up, there must be some other, more 'mental' reasons.

let's take a look at some other possibilities...

NIGHTS

MONEY WORRIES

'If only I'd married that nice Simon who worked in the city and wore red braces' – so he was a coke head but boy was he rich...

*T*he trouble with getting older is that we would like and need more treats but somehow we can't afford them, therefore we will toss and turn under our duvets fretting about all the money that we've wasted over the years on stupid shoes and braces for our ungrateful children.

£ 'If only the boiler hadn't broken down in 1998'

£ 'If only he'd had a better job'

£ 'If only I could be living in a holiday home under Tuscan skies instead of listening to squirrels chew through the electrics'

But hold on, maybe there is light at the end of the tunnel, (or even sleep), why not let us here at *Wendy* help with your money worries.

we're surprisingly clever

Solutions to money worries

SLEEPLESS NIGHTS

No.1

Check you haven't got any odd accounts that you've forgotten about, like some post office savings. You never know, the receptionist here once found an old Chelsea Building society book that contained £7.34!

BECOME A JAM MILLIONAIRE!

Make some jam, put it into jam jars, add a fancy label and maybe a country-style gingham lid and ask Harrods to buy your jam for ten pounds a jar. Might work, might not. If you don't know how to make jam, buy the cheapest jam you can find and decant it.

No. 2

SIGN UP WITH A MODEL AGENCY!

Sometimes they need very ordinary / ugly people for advertising campaigns. You might make a few hundred quid every couple of years

Now that we've given you some ideas to help solve your financial worries, let's think about some other things that are keeping you wide awake at bed time.

Without doubt, one of the most common worries is 'What do I do about the house?'

well, let's explore it...

£100 x ? years =

Doreen x xx

HOUSE WORRIES?

SLEEPLESS NIGHTS

NORMALLY go something like this: 'Should I downsize now that the children are leaving the nest?'; 'Should I stay here in case mother needs to move in?'; 'Should I not stay here in case mother wants to move in?'; 'Is that funny smell in the kitchen damp or a dead rat behind the swing bin?'; 'Have I locked the back door?'; 'Is the chimney going to fall off the roof and kill me or next door's cat?'; 'Maybe the house was built on an ancient burial site or a place where they chucked the palsied bodies of plague victims';

'What does he bloody do in that shed all day?'; 'What happens if that brown patch turns out to be dry rot, and when did we last have the gutters looked at?'; 'When the water mains burst will I remember where the tap is?' (Even though you wrote it down somewhere really safe and important in case of emergencies). What if, what if, what if… is there no peace?

SOLUTIONS TO HOUSE WORRIES

Sell! Don't ever buy anything ever again! So what if you die in rented accommodation, if no one finds your corpse then the landlord's going to just have to deal with it.

Become a matron at a boarding school – unfortunately, it will involve pretending to be nice to other people's children which may prove impossible.

If your kids have left home, move in with them. That'll teach them! Remember when they put your shoes down the toilet and scribbled all over the walls? Well, let's see how they like it! It's payback time.

Go properly mad. Before you know it you'll be tucked up in a nice secure unit and no one will bother you for the rent.

Go and stay with an old schoolfriend… for ever. Choose one that used to bully you as she'll feel too guilty to chuck you out. Aha, revenge is best served by sitting in someone else's conservatory drinking their sherry!

Now that we've helped with your housing worries, let's have a quick Q & A to tackle another possible cause of your insomnia (medical term for sleeplessness). Your health.

HEAL+H

A quick no nonsense Q and A

worries

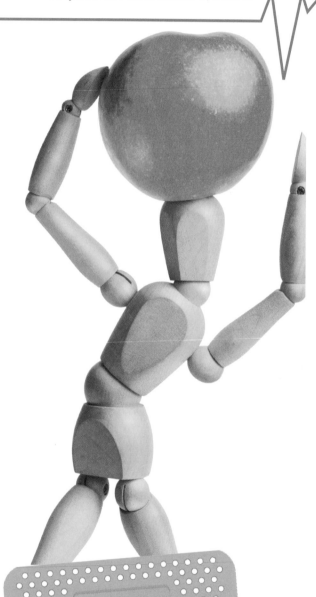

Q AM I TOO FAT?
A PROBABLY.

Q AM I DYING?
A YES, WE ALL ARE, BUT NOT JUST NOW.

SLEEPLESS NIGHTS

Q WILL MY TEETH FALL OUT?
A YES IF YOU DON'T FLOSS.

Q DOES MY HAIR LOOK STUPID?
A ONLY FROM THE BACK.

AND IF YOU'RE NOT WORRYING ABOUT YOUR OWN HEALTH, ODDS ON YOU'RE WORRYING ABOUT YOUR FAMILY'S MENTAL AND PHYSICAL WELLBEING?

WENDY SAYS

KIDS worries

SLEEPLESS NIGHTS

Where are they?

 None of your business.

 What are they doing?

 You don't want to know.

 Will I have to pay the fine?

 Why not make them go halves.

 Is it going to spoil Xmas, my birthday, their life?

 Yes.

Parent Worries

Q: WHAT ARE THEY DOING?
A: THEY'RE NOT SURE.

Q: WHERE ARE THEY?
A: THEY'RE NOT SURE.

Q: HAVE THEY GIVEN IT ALL TO CHARITY?
A: A BIT.

Q: HAVE THEY SPENT THE LOT?
A: QUITE A LOT OF IT.

And now that your health, house and money problems have been dealt with let's try and get you some sleep. Here's a quick hitlist of activities that are bound to send you off (provided your husband isn't roaring beside you).

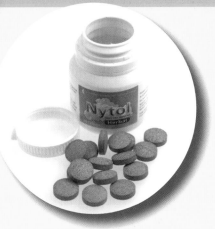

Pills
No more than two
Nytol, mind.

Count sheep

Read a boring book
Anything that's won the
Booker prize over the
past ten years.

Alcohol
Anything red should
knock you out!!

Sex
You might not feel like it but once it's over
you'll be really pleased you did it, bit of
exercise, quite a nice sensation, plus he's really
happy and afterwards he won't mind having a
little chat where you can tell him all your worries
and because he's just had some nice rumpy-pumpy,
he will promise you everything is going to be all right,
snnnnnnnnnnn…

If all fails, get up walk
on cold floors in bare
feet have a banana and
a digestive biscuit.

DREAMS DREAMS DREAMS

analysis

Zandra Wienerschnit-Black

A special by our resident head shrinker, Zandra Wienerschnit-Black.

In my 30 years of clinical experience in Jungian and Freudian therapy, women of a certain age dream remarkably frequently and remarkably vividly.* Interpreting these dreams can unlock some of their innermost fears and desires and can be a short cut to a healthier ego and alter-ego – which in turn may make them easier to live with.

Sigmund Freud is considered to be the father of psychoanalysis and his groundbreaking book *The Interpretation of Dreams* (1913) stated that all dreams have their subconscious meanings, that none of it was accidental, and that our true feelings surface in our dreams whereas awake they are suppressed.

Hence dreaming of being on a picnic in a sunny daisy filled field with an amorous Philip Glenister may mean that the patient secretly wants to shag Philip Glenister. And the good news is that I can charge them about £400 for that piece of information.

Sometimes dreams are tricky to interpret, and other great

psychological masters may come into play. Jung, who studied under Freud (not like that), believed that dreams were significant because they were a window not just on our innermost desires and fears, but our

spriritual side as well, and that they point to good/evil, love/hate, ego and counterego. He suggested that dreams could point the way to how we should solve problems in our real life.

For instance, a patient may come into my very lush and expensive consulting rooms and tell me about a dream about being in the kitchen surrounded by sharp knives which they have an inexplicable desire to sink into their husband's torso as he has just walked in from the garden with mud on his shoes again and left marks on the kitchen floor. Jung would say that this is the patient's counterego telling her that the solution to her problem is to murder her husband. I can't tell her exactly that because I would get struck off, but I can slowly over a long period of (expensive) sessions lead her to this conclusion.

Now, let's take a look at some common dreams of the women of a certain age and see if there's not a few more husbands out there who need murdering.

** Especially after some of that cheap white wine or calvados which was the only thing they could find in the cupboard while watching **Location Location***

Dreams of teeth falling out

A classic anxiety dream that 80% of women and 63% of men will encounter at some time in their lives. This is often a recurring dream that will frighten the pants off you and have you checking to see if your molars are intact in the morning. It's all about losing control to the point that you feel that you are incapable of taking on anything that needs a good metaphorical 'chew', be it a new job or a kitchen extension.

Discuss your worries with your partner, friend or the cat, tackle the problem that you are worried about and be assured that even if you fail badly and publicly humiliate yourself, even if the project (whatever it is) flops dramatically and you are staring financial ruin in the face, your teeth won't fall out in real life. However, just to be on the safe side visit your dentist and make sure you haven't got some dreadful gum disease.

Dreaming of your best friend's husband

Many women dream about their best friend's husband, particularly if you have shared holiday villas together and you have seen him in his trunks. There is no subconscious to this dream: you fancy him and given the chance, you'd like to get your mitts on him. This dream is harmless as long as you don't try turning it into a reality – remember – just because you are dreaming of him, doesn't mean to say he is dreaming of you. He isn't. He's dreaming of Keira Knightley.

Dreams of falling

A classic anxiety dream. This one is about losing status or falling off your pedestal. People normally have falling dreams when they are doubting their own abilities or think they've gone off the boil a bit.

OK, let's get our thinking caps on. Are you rubbish at your job? If you're not sure, lock yourself in a cubicle in the ladies' toilets at work and wait for your colleagues to start bitching about you. Sometimes it's better to know what you're doing wrong so that you can put it right rather than floundering around, upsetting everybody by mistake. If it's not work, then it's probably something that's gone off kilter in the home. Maybe you've put on some weight and you're worried that he no longer thinks you're a goddess. This is easy to check. Just look in the mirror – if you don't like what you see, why should he?

Dreams of being naked

This dream means that you are feeling vulnerable at the moment and a bit exposed. They are often played out in very public places, in front of lots of people. It could be that you're nervous about an event that's coming up, perhaps a presentation to do at work or an important speech to make. Don't worry, the dream won't come true, not unless you're a bit mad and secretly this naked business is not a dream but a fantasy and you're a raving exhibitionist. In which case, go with the flow. Take your clothes off and be proud of your nakedness – however be aware that there are public decency laws you may well be flaunting and gay men might cry at the sight of you.

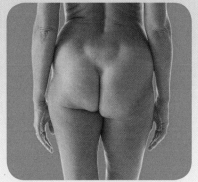

Dreams of making an Oscar acceptance speech

Oh grow up, it's not going to happen. The only thing this dream signifies is that you think you're it. Well, wake up and smell the mould that's coming from the cupboard under the stairs. Dreaming about Hollywood stardom is one thing, but if you think it's going to come true, then you're delusional and should probably speak to a medical expert. Unless of course you're young and beautiful in which case anything is possible, damn you.

RAINY DAY IDEAS

Sometimes the weather can really let us down. We all know how disappointing it is when we are looking forward to a picnic in a park only for our plans to get rained off at the last moment. But don't just sit by the window shaking your fist at the clouds, do something with your rainy day.

Why not make your own star chart?

Take a piece of paper and along the top of the paper divide it into days of the week then put the names of your family down the left-hand side. When (and if) your family have deserved it, award them a gold star and stick it on the relevant day. At the end of the week the person with the most stars should get a treat, like a packet of Maltesers or a Walnut Whip.

If you find that your family are reluctant to join in and are spoiling it for everyone else, award yourself all the gold stars in the packet and then the Maltesers and the Walnut Whip are yours, all yours!

...ay	Monday	Tuesday	Wednesday	Thursday	Friday
...d your body ...rom out of ...he bath! :)	Filling the car up with petrol, rather than leaving me with one measly drop to get to the supermarket.	Playing music at a sociable level. / Taking a message and writing it down, rather than just ...bothering.	Putting empty cereal packets in the bin, not back in the cupboard. / Picking up your shoes. / Being nice to each other and not calling each other names like 'you fat pig!'	Saying please and thank-you instead of taking everything that I do for you for bloody granted.	yum yum all mine! / ME! / Because I do every thing anyway!

Not wasting ...paper.

Tidy out your underwear drawer
(and possibly embark on a new career as a result!)

Be ruthless. Chuck out anything that has got a wretched-looking gusset or bits of lace hanging off. Throw out that thong that you keep thinking might come in useful – it won't. If you're not sure what to keep and what to reject, imagine being in a road traffic accident wearing the questionable garment. If you blush at the thought, chuck it.

Now with all those discarded tights socks and pants, why not make some puppets? Sew on some button eyes and if you're feeling really adventurous, attach some 'wool' hair. Your puppets might be so successful that you will be inspired to write a show for small children which you could perform at parties for a fee.

If you are contemplating this, just remember, as a children's entertainer you are not allowed to hit or shout.

Try to get around the sitting room, without touching the floor

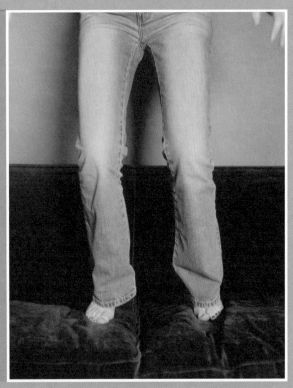

This game is best played with friends. All you need to do is use the furniture and your imagination to get around the sitting room without touching the floor. Imagine the fun that can be had from seeing your plump pal trying to jump between the sofa and the coffee table.

It's best to take your shoes and socks or tights off before embarking on this game – a slippery sole could lead to concussion.

```
M O U S T A C H E W H I S K E R S E R S
X T W E E Z E R S T E D H Q S Z H
Y B G R V T O I B L I P W A X Q R
H E H D E Q C X E H A S O G R S C
O D A I Z P S W J T M C R U Z H H
T C Y S T I T I S O G K K S A O I
F E X H J L B O T R L Y Q S W D R
L O B Y U E N T Y E X J A E L D O
U N U T Z S O C G Q V E X T B Y P
S P S K L B Z O K N Y L W T A R O
H W Y F T P R O P E R L Y S Y H D
A R B N H B N E Y T A Y W N B Z I
G T O X I R W T R S L I P P E R S
V R D F S A C N A G B A G Q D U T
F Z Y T N Q Y X U S E N S I B L E
```

FIND THESE SADLY FAMILIAR WORDS

HOT FLUSH   SLACKS   MOUSTACHE   BUSY BODY   FIBROGEL

DISHY   WHISKERS   PILES

PROPERLY   TWEEZERS   NAGBAG   LIPWAX

SENSIBLE   GUSSETTS

SHODDY   KY JELLY

SLIPPERS   CYSTITIS

FRONT BOTTOM   CHIROPODIST

COLOUR BY NUMBERS

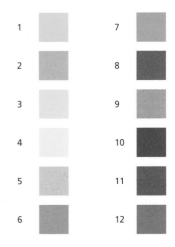
A whole page of rainy day colouring-in for you to while away the waiting hours at the doctor's or the dentist's or even at a train station.

1		7	
2		8	
3		9	
4		10	
5		11	
6		12	

Remember the health benefits of colouring-in are numerous – whilst you are busy with your crayons you will not buy that chocolate bar or pick your face, or do that embarrassing thing which involves tugging out stray eyebrow hairs and then holding them up to the light to see how 'juicy' the root is!

Ideal for the woman who is trying to give up smoking – it could save your life!

If you do a particularly good job, you might be tempted to cut this page out and frame it and perhaps give it to a friend or daughter-in-law.

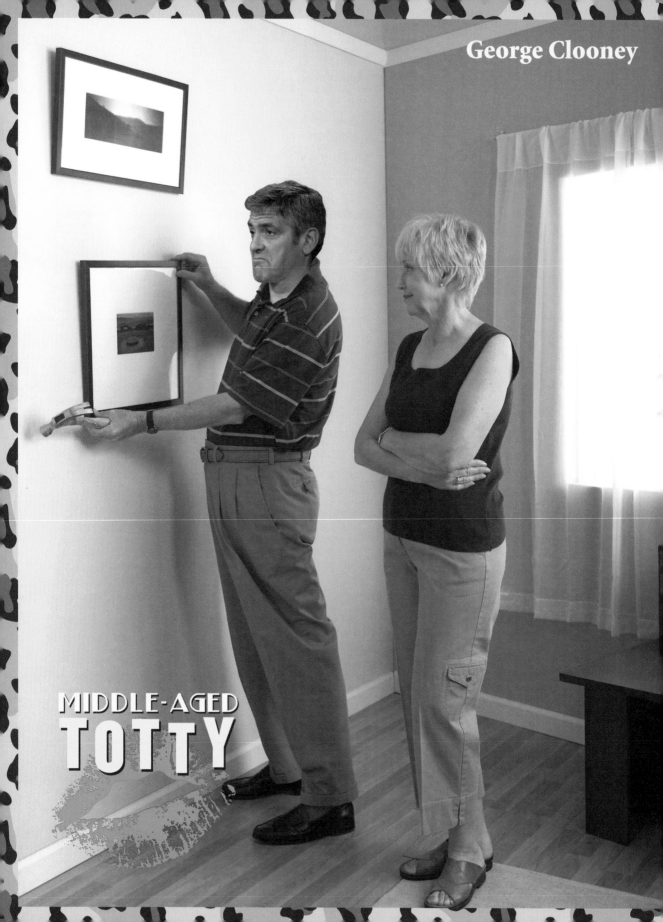

Daniel Craig

MIDDLE-AGED
TOTTY

What Your Shopping Basket Says About You

Green, mean, or fashion queen? **Poison Ivan**, our Hessian Hitler, lets loose on your choice of shoulder accessory.

TESCO CARRIER

Oh dear, we are letting ourselves down, aren't we? As we all know, 'we are where we shop,' so if you're going to be carrying stuff around in a placcy bag, at least make sure it's from Marks. Anyway, plastic bags are so last century, haven't you heard? They're slowly strangling the planet, whales are choking to death on them, they're getting entangled in the intestines of seagulls, dolphins are getting their heads stuck in them, they're killer bags – so what does that make you? Deeply unfashionable, that's what! Everyone's gone green, love, get yourself a 'bag for life', preferably one of those 'I am not a plastic bag' bags from Anya Hindmarsh that all the celebs were toting around last season, or if you really want to make a statement, get yourself a Fairtrade Hessian number – pop a yoga mat and one of those trendy coffee flasks in it and Gwyneth Paltrow, eat your heart out.

WICKER BASKET

Well done, you've successfully graduated into a full-blown scary middle-aged lady and you've got the shopping basket to prove it. Part bag, part weapon, the wicker basket is great for pushing other women out of the way at January sales, and just right for standing jam jars in (let's face it, after the wicker basket, jam making is just a matter of time). It can double as a marvellous cover, should you feel tempted to rob a bank or raid a post office. You could go on a shoplifting spree around Waitrose and even if the alarms started screaming as you exited, you'd only have to give them a look, wave your basket in their face, and they'd cower and give in. You're everything this country used to be good at: pushy, no nonsense and a bit of a stroppy old cow. Well done, you are beyond fashion.

MORE OLD BAGS...

HARRODS LAMINATED

SO we're supposed to think you live in Knightsbridge and that you do your daily shopping at Mr Al Fayed's corner shop? This bag tells the world you're a snob from the provinces or worse, Wiltshire, and have no taste whatsoever. Unfortunately for you, Harrods has had it's hey-day and now only tourists and Americans bother with the place. Harvey Nicks is where the true style Nazis go.

ZIP-UP ONES THAT CONCERTINA DOWN TO A BUS PASS THING IN YOUR HANDBAG
(or one of those loathsome bum bags)

Practical, but this serves no fashion purpose. You're not really much of a shopper. Rambler, perhaps?

MARKET STALL ZIP-UP TARTAN

So naff you could almost make it work as a kitsch statement, but only if you're under twenty-five and have an asymmetrical haircut. For the rest of you, the 'fashion slobs' as I call you, this shrieks working-class, northern markets and wet fish wrapped in newspaper, and is the sort of thing that could contain knock-off perfume. So, either you're groovy, young and ironic, or cheap and northern. Have a good look at yourself in the mirror, which one fits the bill?

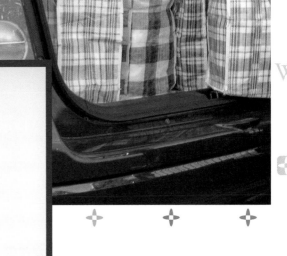

MOCK LEATHER SIT UP AND BEG BAG

Traditionally used by women who catch the bus into town and talk to the person sitting next to them about surgical procedures and 'her' at number 43. Unlike the wicker 'don't-mess-with-me' basket, this bag is more suited to the 'I'm-no-trouble' invisible woman who likes to occasionally sneak under the radar and is forever trying to use out of date coupons to get money off her shopping. This bag will contain a very worn-out purse, some pills to put under the tongue in the event of an angina attack, used hankies and possibly some pick and mix liquorice allsorts that were smuggled in when the security guard had his back turned in Woolies. Ooh, you sneaky old lady.

DANGEROUS
Medical Conditions
YOU NEVER KNEW YOU HAD

Dr RUDOLF CLERC: Staying fit and healthy as we reach our stage in life is crucial to our happiness and well-being (and of the people who live with us). A low fat, high fibre lifestyle with plenty of pomegranates and organic broccoli will go a long way to ensuring that you avoid osteoporosis, obesity, and early onset dementia.

However, there are some lesser known medical conditions that are equally deadly for women of a certain age and we feel it is our duty to reveal to you the symptoms of these most common of conditions.

EXCESSIVE CLEANING DISORDER

(ECD)

All women are born with the Excessive Cleaning Disorder gene, but it generally lays dormant until early adulthood. The condition presents with symptoms of over tidying, needing to make beds, vigorously cleaning already spotless work surfaces and putting on washes before the patient leaves the house in the morning, but can progress to actually gaining pleasure from tasks such as dusting, polishing and vacuuming.

DANGEROUS MEDICAL CONDITION NO. 1

Symptoms include:

- Hating other people cleaning your house because they can't do it properly. This applies particularly to cleaners, who you suspect come to the house, make a lot of calls on your home line, watch some daytime telly, then knock off early because they know you won't be back until much later.

- You clean the insides of the kitchen bin.

- When the old man comes in from the garden saying he has mown the lawn (at last), your first thought is, 'Has he taken his shoes off or has he just walked through the hall with his muddy boots on?'

- Your last job of the day is putting your (kitchen) dishcloth in some bleach in the sink ready for tomorrow.

- Having three different types of cleaning cloth. If you have a traditional yellow duster for dusting brown furniture, a white microfibre cloth for dusting painted surfaces, and a blue microfibre cloth used only for cleaning glass, you are ill. You also have a very clean house.

Cures

Sadly, there is no known cure for ECD. Some have tried shock therapy – living in a student flat during freshers' week or letting your teenage son look after your house while you go away for a weekend break – but results have been inconclusive.

On the flip side, you haven't got ECD if you display any of the following symptoms or behaviour:

- Your ironing pile is more than three days high.

- You use J cloths. J cloths only appeal to men, slovenly women who are not interested in cleaning at all, and students.

- You haven't bought a new mop head in over five years.

- You are an intellectual and don't notice dirt of any kind.

Muttonitis

DANGEROUS MEDICAL CONDITION NO. 2

Muttonitis is a distressing condition, not just for the sufferer herself but for her friends, family and colleagues. Well-meaning acquaintances will attempt to warn the Mutton that she is in danger of embarrassing herself, but pleas for 'toning it down a bit' will fall on deaf ears.

Symptoms

Insisting on dressing at least fifteen (in extreme cases twenty) years younger than she really is. Look out for lots of stonewashed denim and diamante-studded T-shirts that are too tight and too short and expose rolls of dimpled ageing flesh. Looking in a mirror and, much like an anorexic convincing herself that she looks fat, assuring herself she looks fashionable.

Celebrity Muttonitis sufferers may include Madonna and Carol Vorderman and, of course, Nancy Dell'Olio.

Cures

With the benefit of video or photographic evidence, an intervention can be staged to shock the Mutton out of her debilitating condition. Afterwards, she will require a great deal of patience and reassurance from her loved ones as she rehabilitates herself into more suitable garments. It's best not to make the Mutton undertake very drastic changes; small things like being allowed to wear an ankle chain (under slacks) will ease her more comfortably into her new lifestyle. Whatever you do, don't ever say, 'Oh you look nice in that', as this might trigger a relapse into skinny jeans and ankle boots.

NON-STOP BUSY BODYING

A very common condition, especially amongst middle-class mothers with teenage children or anyone who has let themselves go a bit and has a good-looking partner. Most women have a natural tendency towards snooping, it's just that sometimes they get over stimulated and the craving for other people's business can get out of hand.

SYMPTOMS

- Many sufferers can barely wait for their families to leave the house to indulge in a really thorough prying session including suit pocket emptying and 'tidying' – snooping through their children's bedrooms.

- Eavesdropping on conversations of total strangers and offering opinions which might include, 'I'd leave him, you're better off without him' and 'If you ask me, he's seeing someone else'.

- Refusing to be the 'last to know'.

- Taking up the carpet because she thinks there might be a secret diary or a tiny bit of dope hidden beneath the floorboards.

CURES

Some say that chemical intervention is the only answer, but clinical trials suggest that channelling the non-stop busy body's snooping skills into local crime prevention can be very useful indeed. In fact, a new survey suggests that patrolling packs of middle-aged busy bodies in certain areas is cheaper and more effective than guard dogs and security cameras.

Many certain-agers (particularly those with busy-body tendencies) have eyes at the back of their heads and 'don't miss a trick' and, considering they have seen every episode of *Murder She Wrote* and *Waking the Dead*, are walking forensic encyclopaedias. Come on the C.I.D! Get recruiting!

DANGEROUS
MEDICAL
CONDITION
NO. 3

CONSTANT WORRYING

Worrying is natural, especially if you're a woman. However, we mustn't cross the worry border and feel responsible for absolutely everybody and everything all the time.

DANGEROUS MEDICAL CONDITION NO. 4

Life has enough real worries – your hair falling out, having a stroke in the middle of Tesco, your partner being made redundant – so wherever possible, fake ones – chimney falling on your head, being mowed down by and out-of-control double-decker – should take a back seat.

You must also try to find some relaxation time, although it's important to find the right kind of relaxation technique. For example, meditating will inevitably backfire because once you're sitting there cross-legged trying to empty your mind it will invariably fill – like a bucket under a burst pipe – with all sorts of random worries, such as funny smells coming up through the floorboards that might suggest rats and consequently the risk of bubonic plague. The worrier should find a hobby that combines mental concentration with low physical risk, so joining a choir is preferable to a mountain climbing club, or water aerobics over deep-sea diving (especially if one is a bit claustrophobic). Basically, some of us are more suited to life on the spinning tea cups than the Big Dipper.

Symptoms

- Taking a blown-up rubber ring on board a plane with your toddler, just in case the plane comes down over water and in the ensuing panic there is no time to get out your junior life raft.

- Building a barbed-wire fence with search lights round the yew tree down the bottom of the garden because the berries are lethal and bright red. Think how tempting it would be to pop one in your mouth by mistake.

- Keying the air ambulance number into your phone because you know your teenage daughter is going for a nice long walk on a coastal path. Some of those paths are lethal.

- Chest clutching as if in the throws of a heart attack.

- Breathing difficulties that make you sound like a cyborg just because you're running late and may miss your train.

- Crying in the toilets at work because 'you just can't cope'.

- Botox-proof badly furrowed brow.

- Getting halfway into town then coming all the way back because you might have left the bathroom window open.

- Sleeping with a whole load of sheets knotted together under the bed in case there is a fire and you have to leave via the window.

Cures

Happily there are things you can do to calm yourself down:

- Don't eat anything beyond its sell-by date. This should stop you worrying about public attacks of diarrhoea.

- Check the local paper to see if there are any escaped murderers in your area before setting off to take your library books back.

- Do not, under any circumstance, accept a lift on the back of a really big motorbike or a helicopter.

Of course, the biggest worry for a worrier is knowing how much worry is normal. To stop those hands from shaking, we've created our own special Wendy guide line:

Wendy guide line:

Normal

Not Normal

Worrying about your teenage daughter being out at two o'clock in the morning is normal.

Having regular check-ups is normal.

Wearing a bicycle helmet for cycling to the shops is normal.

Wearing goggles when doing a bit of soldering is normal.

Ringing the pub when your husband is twenty minutes late is normal.

Worrying about the boiler giving off toxic fumes is normal.

Worrying about the dog dying of old age is normal.

Keeping an eye on your grandchild in case he puts anything silly in his mouth is normal.

Running around all the clubs in your nightie screaming and crying trying to fnd her is not normal.

Checking yourself for lumps on public transport is not normal.

Wearing a bicycle helmet for walking to the shops is not normal.

Wearing goggles when sewing on a button is not normal.

Phoning the police is not normal.

Sleeping on the roof just in case is not normal.

Having your relatively young dog put down because you don't want to go through that grief is not normal.

Giving your grandchild the Heimlich manoeuvre every twenty minutes is not normal.

It's all a question of degrees and not doing stuff in public that makes other people think that you're a bit mad.

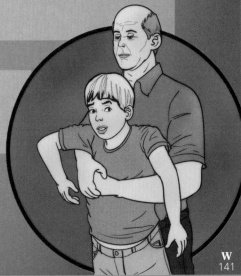

CLEVER CLOGS

Occasionally, we like to get on our high horse and complain about how badly teenagers spell or how illiterate Saturday staff are. But, to keep on feeling superior, and to impress friends/children/potential lovers, we need to constantly top up our knowledge of posh words. Here's a few to get you started.

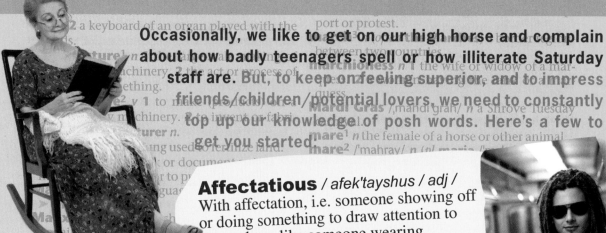

Affectatious / afek'tayshus / adj /
With affectation, i.e. someone showing off or doing something to draw attention to themselves, like someone wearing sunglasses at night. My mother would have called it a gimmick.

Parenthesis / pə'renth☐sis / noun /
If something is in parenthesis, it's in brackets, but with a lot more class.

Postmodern / pohst'modən / adj /
No one knows what it means anyway so just use it willy-nilly and people will nod their heads wisely and pretentiously.

Subtext / subtekst / noun
A neat word because it makes you sound seriously bright and a bit scary. It really only refers to what lies beneath the text, in other words the real meaning of something – when a politician says 'I'm glad you asked me that' the subtext will be 'Christ, I wish you hadn't asked me that!'

Lubricious / looh'brish's / adj /
Fancy word for rude. Comes from the word lubricate – enough said.

Jade Goody
lubricious

WORDY CORNER

Extemporise / *xtemp/pour'ize* / *verb* /
To make it up as you go along, basically the same as 'improvise', but not many people know that, which is why it's such a good word. You can extemporise with things you find in the fridge, but not in a rude way, ladies!

Moribund / *moor'e'bund* / *adj* /
Almost dead. It's a great word to use when you come home on a Friday night, having just done a massive Tesco shop: 'God, I am completely and utterly moribund.' Of course, the danger is that he won't know what you're talking about and therefore won't understand that you are in a state of utter collapse and in desperate need of a cup of tea/gin and tonic/biscuit.

Litigious / *lit'ig'us* / *noun* /
Someone who is prone to taking other people to court. These people can come in two forms: mad old people who write a lot of letters of complaint on Basildon Bond notepaper with a lot of huffing and puffing and won't come to anything, or the really dangerous ones like footballers and celebrities who can afford to take the *Daily Mail* to court for suggesting they might have a small penis or pockets of unsightly cellulite.
Confused? It doesn't matter, just use the word and move on.

Zeitgeist / *zite'gyste* / *noun* /
This is of German origin, and slipping foreign words into your conversation is good as it means you are brainy in more than one language, *ça va* (French for 'innit'). It means fashionable for now, so... Footless tights are zeitgeisty and so is Tracey Emin. Confused? It doesn't matter, just use the word and move on.

Mellifluous / *melli'flewus* / *adj* /
A nice word to use since virtually no one really knows what it means. It's something to do with mellow, sweet, fragrant – nice if you can use it to describe things other than the obvious, such as mellifluous person, mellifluous music, mellifluous conversation, rather than about flowers or honey or anything that gives away the context; that way you keep everyone guessing and retain the intellectual high ground. Marvellous.

Dilettante / *dili'tanty* / *noun* /
Someone who doesn't knuckle down to anything but fiddles about with lots of things. Will probably apply to a younger sibling.

Wendy's Short Stories

HOUSE SWAPPING

I'd always fancied the house next door. It isn't that it's a bit nicer than ours, it's a lot nicer. Don't get me wrong, it's not any bigger, it's just ours had been pebble-dashed back in the sixties and consequently it's a bit of a dingy-beige.

Next door is a nice cheerful Victorian red brick and they have a lovely magnolia tree in the front garden and I do like a magnolia.

On the inside the houses are mirror images of each other, three bedrooms, main bathroom, living room, downstairs WC and kitchen, nothing terribly exciting. There are thousands of semis exactly the same all over the country, just as there are thousands of marriages just like mine and Victor's.

Victor and I have been married for nearly thirty years, happily for about ten, but the last couple of decades have been a bit of a struggle, to be honest. But we soldiered on; we had the twins to think of.

Of course, it's harder when the kids leave home and you realise that you've only got each other left to talk to and you have a horrible feeling that you might have run out of conversation some time back in 1993! So it was quite exciting to see the board go up, it gave us something to chat about.

'I see next door is up for sale,' I said over our supper of lamb chops (too much bone and not enough meat – bit like my marriage in some respects).

Vic muttered something from behind the evening paper.

'I wonder how much it'll go for?'

He muttered something else I didn't catch and went back to reading.

I phoned the estate agent!

'Four hundred and twenty-five thousand,' he said. 'I can arrange a viewing if you like.'

It was strange going round there. We'd not been very friendly with the previous owner. She was a difficult woman and didn't want any interference. I'd tried, but she'd always just shut the door in my face.

'The old lady who lived here died and left everything to a cats' home, no kids, no family. Of course the house needs a bit of sorting out.'

The estate agent was a young lad with a floppy fringe and ridiculously pointed shoes.

I laughed. 'A bit of sorting out? It's a pit!'

He laughed too. 'Just needs someone with a bit of imagination.'

I sighed. 'It needs a damn good clean first.'

And it did, it stank of cats' wee and despair; the house needed some love.

I asked Vic. I said, 'What about we buy next door? Be nice to have a big project we could do together, get stuck in, the two of us.'

Vic looked at me as if I was mad. 'I'm semi-retired, Karen, the only thing I want to do in my spare time is play golf.'

I wanted to tell him I was a bit bored. Since the twins had left for university I had too much time on my hands. I worked three days a week at the stationery shop in the village, but it wasn't enough. I was younger than Vic, I wasn't ready to do 'nothing' just yet.

The 'Sold' board went up about three weeks later. A nice couple in their fifties had bought it, they were downsizing. 'The kids have left home,' said Alan, 'but I fancied a project. I'm a self-employed carpenter and I thought, well, why not?'

His wife Hilary was less enthusiastic. 'I didn't want to do it,' she told Vic. They'd come over for a drink. I was determined to be a better neighbour this time around. 'I don't like mess,' she went on, 'I'm asthmatic.'

So is Vic, and that gave them a lot to chat about. Alan and I talked about colour schemes and his idea for the kitchen extension. 'Why don't you come round and see the plans?' he asked.

So the next day, I did. Hilary wasn't in, she'd gone to stay with her sister for a month while Alan did the dirty work. 'Her nerves,' he explained, 'all the mess makes her anxious.'

I just got used to popping by. With Hilary at her sisters, I'd drop a bit of supper over, and if Vic was playing golf, I'd maybe stay and have a glass of wine. Suddenly I knew that when Hilary came back, things would change and I wouldn't like it.

She did come back, of course, but the plaster and brick dust made her cough, so she would come round to ours. 'I'm sorry, Karen,' she'd say, 'but I just can't stand it, the noise and the smell. I hope you don't mind.'

'Not at all,' chuckled my husband and he always let

'I'd tried, but she'd always just shut the door in my face.'

her choose what we watched on the telly. They liked wildlife programmes, so that was another thing they had in common: wildlife, asthma and jigsaw puzzles. They started piecing together one of a big tiger on our dining-room table.

Now, I'm too impatient for jigsaws, I'd rather be doing something more active. One particularly frustrating evening when I'd been given the tiger's tail to work on, Hilary said, 'Why don't you go and help Alan? He's painting the bathroom. I can't help, just the smell of the paint gives me such a head.'

Victor made a sympathetic noise and offered her some Solpadeine; the two of them were the world's biggest pill poppers.

'And we've still got a long way to go with that jigsaw'

So I did. I went and helped Alan. We painted the bathroom a lovely pale blue and we had a laugh. Then he showed me some more colour charts for the bedroom and I said, 'That pink's nice' and he said, 'Not as nice as you' and the next thing I knew we were kissing.

I went home covered in pale blue paint. Vic didn't notice, in fact he seemed a bit hot and bothered.

'I, I think I'm coming down with something,' he stuttered. 'Maybe I should sleep in the spare room.'

It was a relief not to have to sleep with Vic. I hoped he'd get proper flu and I'd have a week alone in our double bed dreaming of Alan who was just the other side of the wall.

As it was I never slept with Vic again. About three days later he was still in the spare room and I really hadn't seen very much of him. Of course now, looking back, I realise he was avoiding me but at the time I would never have believed the reason why, not until I saw what was happening with my own eyes.

It was a Thursday night, I'd promised Alan a hand finishing the tiling in the kitchen, and as usual Hilary came round to ours. 'It's so peaceful and tidy,' she gushed.

'And we've still got a long way to go with that jigsaw,' added Vic.

I couldn't wait to get out, but ten minutes later I was back. Alan had mislaid his spirit level and I thought we had one in the garage. It was about eight o'clock and just getting dark. The garage is on the left side of our house, and as I walked down the drive I just happened to glance through the window into the dining room where my husband was passionately kissing Hilary. They were really going for it, pieces of jigsaw were spilling off the table and both of them had taken off their glasses.

I celebrated by rushing straight back round to tell Alan – who promptly opened a bottle of wine before making love to me on the newly carpeted sitting-room floor.

In the end it was all very civilised. Hilary moved into my house and I moved into hers. The children were a bit shocked at first, our twins and Alan and Hilary's three boys, but as I told our two, 'You don't want us interfering in your lives, so don't expect to meddle in ours.'

They took it quite well.

The one compromise we did make was that Alan and I moved into the spare room at the back of the house. There is something rather off-putting about lying in bed at night knowing that both your ex-partners are almost within touching distance! Especially as, if we were really quiet, we could hear them – watching a wildlife documentary!

THE END

ARE YOU EASY TO GET ON WITH?

As we all know, women are the more reasonable of the species, but then again some of us are more reasonable than others. Whatever you do, don't let anyone else in your family do this quiz for you!

When he spills tea on the carpet, do you...

A) Go to bed for a week and sulk?
B) Instantly take off your skirt and use it to mop up the stain, thereby ruining your skirt but saving the carpet?
C) Get busy with a tea towel?
D) Bung a copy of *TV Quick* on top of the puddle, which with any luck will soak up the stain? If not, you can shift the furniture round.

He's lost his mobile phone. Do you...

A) Go to bed for a week and sulk?
B) Give him yours and then go out searching the streets for his, putting up missing posters on lampposts?
C) Dial his number and hear it ringing in the pocket of his gardening jacket, which is in the cupboard under the stairs?
D) Think 'So what!' because you lost yours too when you were bit pissed at lunch time?

He's promised to take you out for a meal but at the last minute decides he has to visit his best friend in hospital. Do you...

A) Go to bed for a week and sulk?
B) Instantly make a home-made card and a fruit cake for the friend who is sick in hospital and promise to spend the evening on your knees praying for the patient's speedy recovery?
C) Offer to drive him to the hospital and go out for dinner afterwards?
D) Not care less. You can't actually remember his mate's name and besides, you'd rather be in eating fried chicken out of a bucket in front of the telly than going to some poncy restaurant where they won't let you have a fag?

Answers

Mostly As: At least you're predictable. The thing is, sulking achieves absolutely nothing except a stupid donkey expression. Pull that lower lip back and face up to your problems. Nothing gets solved by hiding under the duvet.

Mostly Bs: We're surprised your skin hasn't turned into coconut matting. You're a complete doormat! Pull yourself together woman, you're a martyr and your entire family are taking you for a ride. Pretend to be dead and see if they take any notice.

Mostly Cs: Congratulations, you're normal. Rest assured your family would fall apart without you. You deserve a treat – put your feet up and have a nice sticky bun. Well done you.

Mostly Ds: If there's one thing worse than a martyr, it's a slob. You really are a slovenly pig. In fact you are so slutty, we're a bit jealous. Well done for not having those tedious responsibility issues that most middle-aged women suffer from. Mind you, we bet your house stinks.

HUBBY PIN-UP

Slightly disappointed with the man you ended up with? We have the solution. Pop your fella's face in the spaces provided and your disappointment at having married him might fade. Then again it might make it worse.

A. SUCCESSFUL HUBBY PIN-UP   **B. FIT HUBBY PIN-UP**

A
Stick Hubby's
Face Here

B
Stick Hubby's
Face Here

MEN AND FASHION

Why aren't they ALL like David Beckham?

Left to their own devices men wouldn't buy any new clothes until the year after next. Consequently, women like us have to take control.

Of course, these days we don't just have to worry about how we look, there's always the chance (a big one) that the old man might be letting the side down in public. Have a good look at your fella; are you positive that if you didn't want him, anyone else would?

The trouble with men is that if they're left to their own devices they can do some very peculiar things. This is why they must be accompanied when shopping at all times.

It's our duty as interfering wives/ life-partners of the world to step in and say, 'I wouldn't be seen dead with you wearing that'. However, if you want to avoid a domestic confrontation, it's a good idea to 'lose' some of his clothing behind his back.

Start by getting everything of his out onto the bedroom floor and sorting it into three piles – passable, charity shop and bin. Put all the passable stuff back in the wardrobe and load the car up with the rest and deal with it. Claim there was a localised fire in the bedroom – you are lucky to be alive – and you had to throw it all out because it stank of smoke. Gosh, what a lucky escape. He may be suspicious, but you will have to be economical with the truth – after all you are doing it for his own good. You may want to salvage from 'the fire' one pear of his baggy jeans and a jumper for all those Little Jobs you are going to give him.

WHAT ON EARTH DOES HE LOOK LIKE?!

INSERT YOUR FACE HERE

If he's got a job where he has to wear a suit, shirt and tie, you can breathe a sigh of relief (assuming that you keep an eye out for any novelty ties, braces or socks). But at the weekend and on holiday, a man and his wardrobe can find true expression, and bring shame on your good family name.

SOME SARTORIAL CRIMES THAT MEN ARE PRONE TO COMMIT:-

❖ Trousers too short, showing horrible white socks.

❖ Anything a bit punky.

❖ Something that suggests that in his imagination he is a cowboy. One tiny bit of cowboy is forgivable – cowboy boots worn discreetly under jeans (not with jeans tucked in) – but once he even looks at a Stetson you're in trouble.

❖ Jogging bottoms worn with office shoes.

❖ Disney ties.

❖ Very tight jeans that show the shape of his willy.

❖ Nylon football strip.

❖ The Iron Maiden roadie look.

❖ Anything his mother bought/knitted for him.

❖ Skate-boarder clothes on anyone over thirty-five.

❖ Offensive slogans on T-shirts.

❖ Sandals – very tricky for a man of a certain age. Especially beware Jesus sandals, or anything too strappy, or made out of burst tyre.

❖ The dreaded three-quarter-length socks and shorts combo.

❖ The thinning hair – get him to cut it, not wear a baseball cap.

❖ Short-sleeved shirts. Doesn't matter how clever you are, this is a look that takes hundreds of points off your IQ.

❖ The anorak – burn it or hide it.

❖ Speedos. Oh my god. No.

Solutions

When confronted with any of the fashion barbarity mentioned above, there can only be one course of action:

1. March him down to Next/M and S/Debenhams (bribe him with sexual favours if you must). If he starts struggling in the curtained off cubicle, get down on your knees. Prayers don't work, you know what will.

2. Tell him you'll pay for it all. Even if you use his card.

3. Praise him. It will work wonders.

NB Make sure you don't make him look too good otherwise that cow that works with him who sometimes texts him at weekends is going to take a real fancy to him. Things could backfire.

Remember, when taking all his horrible clothes to the charity shop, make sure you donate them to a worthy cause in the next town. The last thing you want is him recognising his holiday shorts in the window of your local Sue Ryder and rebuying them. For some reason, men get ludicrously attached to the most hideous items of clothing.

WENDY SAYS

CUT & PASTE SOME ESSENTIAL

Why not take some time to cut these outfits out and spend a few hours dressing our 'everyday bloke'. That way you might get some idea of how stylish your husband could look (if you tried hard enough).

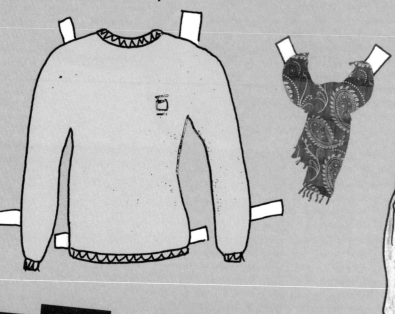

- ❖ A nice pair of corduroy trousers, cord jacket stripey shirt, selection of navy and white t-shirts
- ❖ Roomy jeans linen jacket, pinstripe jacket, paisley scarf
- ❖ Stripes – very good on a man, especially once the wrinkly neck starts
- ❖ Baggy boxer swimming trunks – especially good with flowery patterns or in pink – man in touch with his feminine side
- ❖ Leather jacket – but not a bomber jacket – too young
- ❖ Trainers – definitely not in white
- ❖ Tracksuit – only when jogging emphatically. Not even for going to get the Sunday papers in

WARDROBE ITEMS FOR THE MAN IN YOUR LIFE

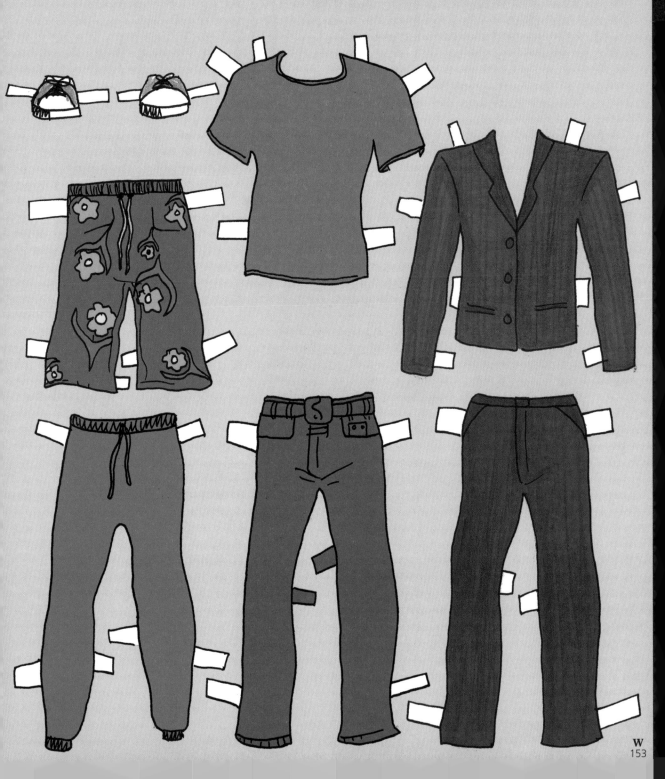

AFFAIRS
should you or shouldn't you?

Most of us at some point will consider having an affair. It might be that someone at the PTA pays you more attention than your beloved (not hard), and your sex life is staler than bread that's not fit for throwing at ducks. Whatever the reason, it's inevitable that over the course of a marriage, the eye, and maybe the hands, will wander.

So should you or shouldn't you? We've outlined some of the major pros and cons for you to tick off as a checklist * whilst you weigh it up; but the truth is you won't take a darn bit of notice if you really want one, you hussy.

* Whatever you do, don't leave this checklist lying around the house. If you're going to be unfaithful, you're going to have to get sneaky.

Why you should

- You'll stop being such a lardy pants – having sex with someone new is notoriously good for shifting the weight, unless he's a Polish truck driver or runs a chippie.
- You will probably have to have sex in hotel rooms, which means you can nick all the little soaps and sachets of hair conditioner from the bathroom.
- Some of your friends will be really jealous, particularly if you lie and say he's a tennis instructor. Ha, that's one in the eye for Alexandra Braithwaite who might have a new kitchen but hasn't got a (fictional) tennis-pro lover.
- You'll feel so pleased with yourself and have such a spring in your step that you'll forget about that damp patch in the spare room that's come back again despite getting it painted with anti-damp stuff.

Why you shouldn't

- Just think of all that waxing you're going to have to do: legs, undercarriage and moustache – the pain, the pain!
- You'll have to buy some new underwear which will involve having to look at yourself in the mirror while trying stuff on. Yuk.
- You will have to practise and perfect holding your stomach in for hours at a time. Men who have affairs usually aren't getting any nooky at home and therefore want to make a bit of meal of it. You, on the other hand, would like to get it over and done with and then go out for 'something nice to eat'.
- You will have to have the lights off – it's about 15 years since you stripped off in front of someone other than the old man; in which case you might as well do it with the old man.
- Sex won't be all that good until you have done it a few times. Remember when you starting shagging your husband…? Yes, your husband, the one you are betraying right this minute in a horrible Travel Lodge with a nasty purple bedspread, just outside of Nuneaton. Hmmm, is it really worth it?
- You will have to delete all his texts, which means putting your reading glasses on and fiddling about with the mobile.
- You risk your old man finding out and being so jealous he will either leave you or retaliate with your friend Cynthia, who you know has always fancied him. So think about it carefully.
- You won't be able to fart in front of him. If you did, even once, it would cease to become an affair and start to become a 'relationship' so you'll have to hold it all in and you know that's not good for your irritable bowel syndrome. Gaviscon in the handbag is unsexy.

Wendy's Short Stories

MY D.I.V.O.R.C.E.

I'm trying to think whose idea this was in the first place. I think it was probably Sally who said, 'Hey girls, why don't we have a weekend away?'

Course we were all up for it. Joanna wanted to go to some spa for a pamper, but then that's Joanna – her old man's loaded, fits fitted kitchens – but we're not all in the same boat. Ever since Paul left me to bring up our two kids on my own, I've been struggling. Ten years of single parenting isn't easy, especially when your ex just buggers off and the only contact you have is through the CSA.

'I was glad I'd been drinking...'

Still, I could manage a weekend away and the girls are old enough to look after themselves now. Becky's nineteen and Rachel's seventeen. 'No parties,' I told them. I wasn't worried, they're good kids. People say I've done a good job; well, I didn't have any choice. I'd been married nearly ten years and one day he just walked out, no explanation, no forwarding address, no nothing. Just a note with the words 'Even if I told you, you wouldn't understand' scrawled across the paper in blue biro.

In the end us girls decided to go to Blackpool. It was cheap and we could have a laugh and if the weather was good we might even catch a tan. 'Fat chance in October,' said Elaine.

So there were the four of us. We booked two double rooms in the poshest hotel on The Prom; me and Sally in one and Joanna and Elaine in the other.

We came down from Glasgow on the train. It was a direct route and we had a picnic of M&S goodies on the way. I'd have bought my own sandwiches but Joanna insisted that it was her treat, and sometimes it's nice to have a Mediterranean platter and some stuffed vine leaves rather than a boring cheese and tomato butty. She bought us four miniatures of white wine. I think I fell asleep just outside of Carlisle.

That was yesterday, it's Saturday morning now and I'm the only one up. The weather's dreadful and we've all got hangovers. Last night got a bit silly – but then, what do you expect? Four middle-aged women off the leash and on the town.

We ended up in a gay bar where there was a cabaret on. The four of us squashed around a table, drinking vodka and tonics. Silly after all the wine we'd drunk in the hotel restaurant over dinner, but you know what it's like, we felt young again – and then I saw him.

I should say her. She was doing a Dolly Parton act, 'Stand by your man,' she's singing, and I was a bit tipsy and I remember thinking 'I did, I stood by him, he just didn't stand by me', and I caught her eye and I knew. I knew, even though I hadn't seen him for ten years, I knew the transvestite in the blond wig and the silver heels was my ex-husband. It was Paul, and for a moment we just stared at each other, but I swear he never missed a beat.

I didn't know what to do. I was glad I'd been drinking; it stopped me from feeling too shocked.

Paul finished the song and he walked over to the piano and he whispered something into the pianist's ear and then he started singing that Elton John song 'Sorry Seems to be the Hardest Word', and Joanna yelled 'Oy, that's not a Dolly Parton song' but Elaine said 'Shhhhhh, he's got ever such a lovely voice' and he had. I'd only ever heard him sing lullabies to the kids before – I'd never really noticed. The whole club went quiet, I had goosebumps up my spine and all of a sudden I needed to put my cardi back on.

When he finished the crowd went mad. Brenda, Joanna and Sally were shouting 'More, more', but he just got off the bar stool he'd been sitting on and walked offstage. Finally, just before he disappeared through a lurex curtain, he turned, looked me straight in the eye and blew me a kiss and I thought 'Well, at least now he has told me'.

THE END

Easy Clean Lie Detectors

A welcome addition to every kitchen. Just plug in and hey presto you have an easy to use everyday polygraph to sort out domestic arguments/ disagreements once and for all.

Money back guarantee if not entirely satisfied.

...an be disguised as a ...aster tidy for those delicate extra-marital suspicions.

REAR WINDOCULARS

AVAILABLE IN TARTAN

...For those days when only standing at the window and ...staring into other people's lives will do. Comes with ...handy focus puller for those tricky to snoop windows.

MERKIN U LIKE

For the woman with less down there than she used to have. Anchored by new, ultra-smooth, invisible Velcro technology.

Available in blonde, ginger and natural grey.

Machine washable.

SPICING UP YOUR SEX LIFE

✳ ✳

Just Say Yes!

For once JUST SAY YES. The biggest drawback to a healthy sex life is getting a bit lazy and forgetting how much we like a bit of rumpy-pumpy. Eventually you get into such a habit of saying 'NO' and 'I'm tired' and 'I've got a headache' and 'There's good TV on', that we forget that sometimes we aren't and we haven't and there isn't.

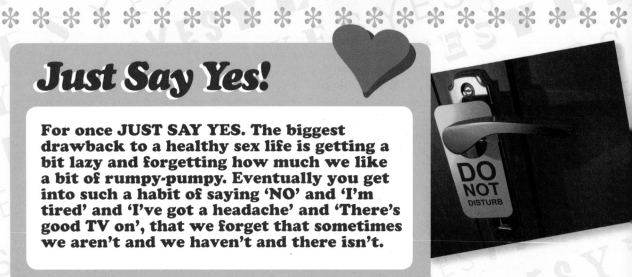

Preparation

Now that you've decided that you're going to say YES, you need to plan this event intricately. The most important thing is relaxation, so an afternoon nap is imperative. If you work and you haven't got the kind of job where you can get away with putting your head down for an hour after lunch (say you operate a till at Asda) tell them you've got a dental appointment and come home early.

Spicing Up Your Sex Life

Food ♥

Tasty, you like that?

OOh yum!

* **Make him something nice, but not too heavy, for tea. We suggest something like tuna steaks on crushed new potatoes with some tiny roast tomatoes for colour. Or beans on toast. It's important to line the stomach before sex, as if you go to bed hungry your body will make all kinds of off-putting growling noises.**

Drinks & Treats ♥

Lovely!

* **Share a bottle of champagne and let him have a small portion of ice cream for pudding. This will let him know that you're in a good mood and that he hasn't done anything wrong – yet.**

Wonderful!

W
159

Foreplay

Squeezing his knee as you breeze gently past will sow the seed of romance. It also officially counts as foreplay.

Then let him watch something he likes on telly. If it clashes with something you want to watch, let it go; he'll be so chuffed after sex later that you'll get telly rights for at least a week.

Go upstairs and have a nice bubble bath. This is the crucial stage, and if anything goes wrong (no hot water, towels are in a filthy heap) try to rise above it and squirt some perfume around your bits and bobs.

'Your father and I are going to have sex tonight.'

Once you're out the bath, go into the boudoir and shut the curtains (especially important if you live on a bus route and there are road works holding up the traffic). If you're worried about the kids getting in the way, make sure they are asleep or out of the house. Teenagers are very easily bribed with a tenner and the quick announcement, 'Your father and I are going to have sex tonight.' Their horror should keep them out your way for at least a week.

Break
A Leg!

LIGHTING & COSTUME

Make sure you're dressed for the occasion. If you haven't got any sexy negligees, make sure you're wearing a nice, clean, fresh nightie and not one of his old vests. Men tend to be turned off by their own smell.

Fantastic!

Men like underwear, so why not dig out that corset you wore when you were in that Restoration drama for the amateur dramatics. If you don't have anything made of satin and lace, don't be tempted to put on the orthopaedic corset – the straight backed posture has never worked.

DON'T TRY TOO HARD

It's all very well pouting, winking and doing the big come hither, but unless you've practised this in a mirror, it could back fire and end with you looking scary and mad. It's best just to smile in a friendly way and not say anything off-putting like, 'Did you put the bins out?'

Kick starting the proceedings

> It's rude to talk with your mouth full.

* **Married men**, or those in long-term relationships, are usually so sex-starved that they will do anything for nookie, but there are those who are so programmed to not getting any that an offer might short circuit them. If your man's an asthmatic make sure his inhaler is nearby, in case your posturing brings on an attack.

* **Do something you know he likes.** Some men like their ears being stroked, some men like a nice bit of snogging, all men like blow jobs. If you opt for the latter don't be surprised if he asks whether it's his birthday and don't spoil the occasion by talking about new kitchens. It's rude to talk with your mouth full.

What to do after

SEX BURNS OFF QUITE A LOT OF CALORIES, SO MAYBE A BISCUIT OR A CHOCOLATE AFTERWARDS WOULD BE NICE. WHY NOT CELEBRATE WITH A CELEBRATIONS CHOCOLATE? KEEP A BOX UNDER THE BED FOR OCCASIONS SUCH AS THIS.

WENDY SAYS

After you've done the sex, you will sleep very well indeed and for once his snoring won't keep you awake. Men find it hard to snore when they've got a big fat grin on their face.

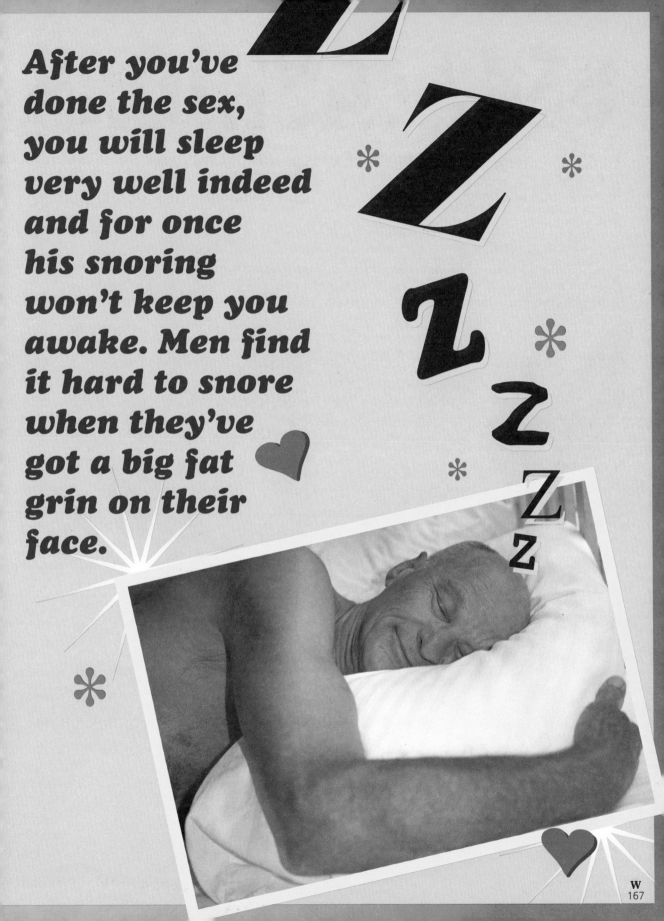

SEXY FASHIONS

FOR THE OVER FORTIES...

Sex shops are full of dressing-up outfits for silly young girls, but tend not to cater for the more voluptuous woman in her forties who has no interest in dressing-up like a naughty school girl or a saucy nurse. No, we need to be more age-appropriate when playing dress-up in the bedroom, so here are some sexy suggestions that you can easily make up out of bits and bobs in your wardrobe.

WHAT DOES THIS HUSSY THINK SHE IS WEARING? YOU COULD TAKE A NASTY TUMBLE IN THOSE RIDICULOUS HEELS.

TRAFFIC WARDEN

This is an easy outfit to cobble together; all you need to do is wear your second-best black suit and a scowl. These days traffic wardens carry digital cameras, so you can use yours in the bedroom photographing any offences that he may commit, such as dribbling on the pillow. Obviously, any bedroom offences will incur fines which can be paid in cash or kind!

STRICT LATIN TEACHER

All you need is some horrible glasses, a pleated skirt some darned green woollen tights and a shapeless cardi. For the sexy corporal punishment bit, buy a ruler from Woolworths and smack him on the hand for forgetting his Latin declensions, this should get you into a complete sexy frenzy.

LOLLYPOP LADY

Best played out when the central heating has broken down as it involves wearing a big waterproof coat complete with a fluorescent bib and peaked cap. Watch what you do with your 'STOP' sign, you don't want to knock down your Lladró figurine collection, so be careful. For advanced role players only.

UNDERCOVER POLICEWOMAN

At our age, if you were in the police force you'd have been promoted by now, so why not be an undercover lady detective? All you need is a beige mac, some unflattering trousers and a caramel coloured crew neck and, Bob's your uncle, you could go anywhere and no one would notice you. Don't get too rough when you're interrogating him, you're role playing, not trying to beat a confession out of him. Mind you, once you've got him handcuffed to a chair you might as well nag out a confession that it was him who accidentally unplugged the freezer in the garage just before Christmas 2003 thus rendering a hundred and fifty quids worth of perishables into mush. If you ask me that deserves a long night in solitary confinement, i.e. the spare room.

WHY WE LIKE A MAN IN UNIFORM

So why do we like a man in uniform?

Women of a certain age find themselves drawn to different type of men as they get older. They no longer like men in flashy sports cars, or men with lashings of blond floppy hair or a man with prospects. Their taste becomes, shall we say, more realistic. After all, a man in his mid-fifties who says he has good prospects is a bit dysfunctional, or delusional, or both. No, these women are much more modest in their requirements, what they want is someone who:

- Washes regularly
- Doesn't have a police record
- Doesn't live with his mother
- Has all or most of his own teeth
- Knows how to unblock a drain

Any man with all or most of these attributes is worth a look at.

If all these requirements are coupled with an ability to cook a cheese soufflé or lemon meringue pie, you may need to double check whether they're gay (plastic-laminated aprons of their own might confirm), but if not, they can be ideal mates and lovers. When we say lovers, it might be more of a companionship thing, someone to go to B&Q with, or share a bag of Doritos with, that kind of thing.

However, if there's one thing that's a universal in the fancying stakes, it's a man in a uniform. Men in uniform have appeal to women from the time of their first groinal stirrings, but it is a condition that seems to get markedly more pronounced with age.

SURGEON

Consultant Surgeon

The green theatre gown, white clogs and seriously magnifying headgear signifies a top consultant. Swoon... It implies financial security and bedside manner – a very good combination. On the downside, the trouble with surgeons is that they know you inside out, literally, and once you realise that he has seen your fanny full-on and your hefty thighs hoisted up by a pair of stirrups then the fantasy starts to lose its appeal.

FIREMAN

Fireman

By definition, firemen are both tough and wonderful human beings – able to rush into a burning house or climb up ladders or cut children free from mangled car wreckage – and are fit in the proper old-fashioned sense of the word. Starting a fire on purpose to get one to rush into your bedroom and throw you over his back is not acceptable, but you could borrow your small nephew and take him to the local open day at the fire station.

Pilot

Used to be up there with surgeons on the hot totty stakes, but since cheap air fares have arrived, the only ones that are really attractive are the long-haul ones, with lots of blue and gold epaulettes and crisp white pilot shirts. It's disappointing that they started closing the door to the cockpit as now we can't see them pulling that big lever thing that they call throttle, which would inevitably bring on hyperventilation.

LIFEGUARD

Lifeguard

Good to look at and admire from afar but you sadly haven't a chance in hell. They go for flicky hair blonde girls with long legs who surf well or don't get their bikinis wet at all. You are likely to be wearing a swimming costume and sarong so be realistic. Forget it.

EXCEPTIONS TO THE RULES

RULE BREAKERS

Traffic Warden

The exception to the uniform rule, traffic wardens are, by definition, unsexy, unattractive and unappealing. We know this for a fact because over the years we have used all our feminine wiles to try and get them to turn a blind eye to our parking transgressions. We have batted our eye-lashes, flirted, limped, cried... and all to no avail. They are all cold-hearted beasts who would be all right if they looked like Heathcliff (or Johnny Depp), but they don't.

Ambulance Man

Ambulance men don't really do it for most of us despite the fact that they are in lots of ways just like firemen – willing to risk their lives to rescue people from hideously dangerous situations. The problem is their uniform is bright green and they're a bit jobsworthy these days, and some of them are women with gender confusion.

Policeman

Don't be ridiculous, they all look about twelve.

ARE YOU A BIT OF A BOSSY BOOTS?

Bossiness is next to godliness, or so the saying goes. We know what we want, know how to get it and aren't going to let anything or anybody stand in our way. We've earned our bossiness, been there, done that, got the Packamac, and we know when we are being underchanged or someone is pulling the wool over our eyes. Ain't no fooling us. The problem is no one listens to us or cares or even sees us and this can lead to control issues.

Answers

Mostly As
Abnormally patient. Are you Mary Archer?

Mostly Bs
Sometimes you need to think before making a great big fuss about something that is out of your control, but on the whole you're getting there.

Mostly Cs
We're guessing you live alone?

To find out how bossy you are try this easy and convenient Quiz:

Do you half-listen to other people's conversations? Say your daughter is on the phone to her best mate and you just happen past the bedroom door whilst dusting the radiators and pick up a few titbits from inside. Would you…

A) Think to yourself 'Gosh, how different young people are today? Bless them, they deserve a break from their studies'.

B) Phone a friend who has a daughter the same age and ask if they have done drugs awareness at school?

C) Look into electronic tagging and lie detectors that plug into the toaster?

You like to leave your work bags by the front door. It's not like you're a fusspot or an over-organiser, it's just that you have easily the worst day ahead of anyone in the house and you won't be able to cope unless you get all of the tasks in those bags done tomorrow. Someone, however, does not understand how important your system is, and accidentally covers one of your bags with their coat, or moves them into the garage. Do you…

A) Not notice until you get to work? Hey, you can take in the dry-cleaning tomorrow instead. No worries.

B) Decide not to make a big thing of it, but resolve to say something tonight at supper?

C) Yell your head off and wake everyone who is not yet up, saying you can't cope with your life and this is the last straw, then go buy some of that yellow and black striped tape to put round important things so that no one will move them ever again?

Your other half has offered to take over the supermarket shopping, which none will argue is a beautiful, loving gesture. Only trouble is he doesn't know a floor wipe from a pack of fresh basil and you have all been eating sirloin steak and chips or microwave lamb bhunas for a month. Do you…

A) Let it lie? He's doing his best and taking some of the pressure off you. Aren't new men wonderful!

B) Praise him but tell him that you are a better shopper than he is and how about you take it back over and he washes the car every week instead, like real men ought to?

C) Go to the shops with him, and then every time he picks up something silly from the shelf and goes to put it in the trolley you casually suggest that some cauliflower might be better, and that you could show him how to make some nice home-made soup, or 'help' him choose some freshly squeezed orange juice or low fat yoghurt?

10 THINGS THAT CAN PUSH YOU OVER THE EDGE

1. Him retuning your car radio so that every ffteen minutes you get traffic news.

2. Having just the one pound coin in your purse that for some reason falls straight through the parking meter. You risk it and get a ticket, even though the only reason why you were illegally parked is because you were taking a load of things to the charity shop.

3. Opening the really high cupboard in the kitchen to be met by a really heavy tin of baked beans falling on your nose, which makes you cry uncontrollably.

4. Being convinced you have black peppercorns somewhere in the cupboard and spending an inordinate amount of time scrabbling past out-of -date cans of peas and carrots to find them, while your meal goes cold and tasteless. You never do find them.

5. Making a big effort to go swimming only to find once you get there it's closed due to some kids' stupid gala.

6. Finding an empty bottle of vodka hidden in your fifteen-year-old daughter's wardrobe, alongside a lighter and some cigarettes and something that could be dope, but might just be rabbit poo.

7. Realising you haven't got a rabbit.

8. Having a new carpet laid and realising two months later that the radiator has been leaking and it's all gone mouldy behind the sofa.

9. Being taken to the theatre for your birthday treat and ending up behind a man with a very large head and a cough. Then the person you've come expressly to see (eg Michael Ball) is announced as ill and the rubbish understudy is on.

10. Your iron spits funny brown juice all over your new cream silk blouse.

I DON'T NEED A DRINK TO ENJOY MYSELF!

*If there's one thing that distinguishes Silly Young Girls from Women of a Certain Age, it's the former's need for a drink or twelve to enjoy themselves. We, on the other hand, do not need a drink to enjoy ourselves. We like a walk in the park, some nice fresh air, the smell of hyacinths, or best of all, some good clean fun in the shape of a good party game. **If you're stuck for some ideas for some good clean fun, here are a couple of ideas to keep up your sleeve that you can rustle up at a moment's notice.***

THE GIDDY KIPPER GAME

For two or more players
Super fun for all ages (as long as you are capable of getting down on your hands and knees).

PREPARATION

Cut out two identical fish shapes from an old newspaper (make a few more just in case).
Roll up the remainder of the newspaper into two batons.
Push all the furniture in the sitting room right back to the wall, making sure there will be enough space to race your fish across the carpet.
Players then get down on their hands and knees in order to 'beat' the fish across the room with the rolled-up newspaper batons. The trick is to create a wafting motion so that the fish literally fly across the room. First one to the other side wins.

This game can be played as a relay team event or, if you're very lonely, by yourself against the clock.

THE PEA-SUCKING GAME

YOU WILL NEED:
Two pyrex pudding bowls, a pack of drinking straws and a box of dried peas.

Put the peas in a bowl and place it on a coffee table alongside an empty one.
Get your guests to take it in turns to kneel on the floor (you may need to do an informal medical here for the over 60s – these days people sue).
Time them for a minute as they suck the peas from the bowl and deposit them into the empty one. Then count up how many they've done. Sounds simple? Try it.

Very fit people can suck so hard that they get more than one pea on the straw at a time. However, the clever pea-sucker doesn't waste precious breath on this, but rather concentrates on perfecting a steady accurate stream with a nice flick at the end.

THE MUSICAL CHAIRS GAME

Ideally a summer game due to obvious breakage potential (furniture and orthopaedic).

Set out your dining chairs or deckchairs and bring the radio outside.
Put less chairs out than people playing and off you go.
Everyone has to walk round without stopping or pausing at chairs.
The moment the music stops everyone has to sit on a chair as fast as possible.
No chair, you're out.
The fewer the chairs the more violent the game gets.
Watch as grown men and women are ready to push, scratch and bully others out of their way to win.
And all for a box of Quality Street.

NB This game can make you laugh so much that you wet yourself. Wear double gussets or Tena lady.

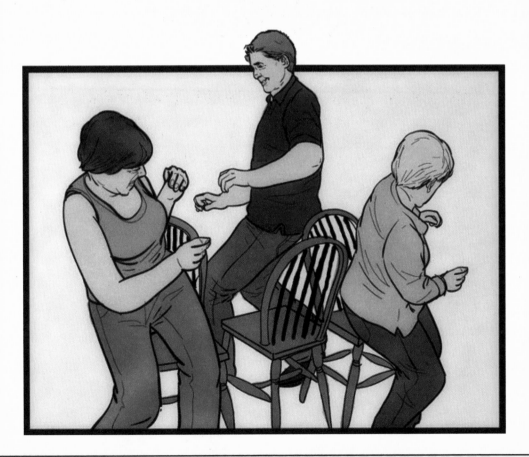

ARE YOU AN ALCOHOLIC?

It's a well-known fact that we can't drink as much as we could. One minute we're writing tomorrow's to-do list, then after a couple of DWW (dry white wines) we're fast asleep in front of the ten o'clock news (again). Try our simple quiz to find out whether your DWW habit is becoming a problem or not.

Q. ARE YOU GOING TO THE BOTTLE BANK WITH DWW BOTTLES...

a) Once a month?
b) Once a fortnight?
c) Every Saturday?

Q. WHEN YOU ARE TOTTING UP YOUR WEIGHTWATCHERS POINTS, HOW MANY DO YOU ALLOCATE OUT OF YOUR DAILY TOTAL OF 18 TO DWW?

a) None – you'd much sooner save them for a Bakewell tart before bed.
b) At weekends, you carry forward 6 for one DWW on a Saturday night.
c) You eat 8 points on food and the rest you save for DWW.

Q. AT A NIGHT OUT WITH THE YOUNG THINGS AT WORK AT CHRISTMAS DID YOU...

a) Make polite conversation but leave early – they don't want you cramping their style and going on to the night club?
b) Let your hair down a little, had a giggle and got home at 10pm, in time for the news, and to get something out of the freezer for tomorrow?
c) Not remember how you got home, and are still dealing with the fallout of all the emails you sent when you logged on pissed out of your mind?

Q. DO YOU ORDER AN EXTRA DRINK FOR YOURSELF WHEN YOU'RE GETTING A ROUND IN?

a) You don't really go to pubs and have never bought a round in your life. Why should you spend money on expensive spirits when all you want is a Britvic orange?
b) You try to avoid buying rounds because you only want the one and it's not really financially viable to buy fifteen drinks and then leave.
c) Yes, you usually order yourself an extra DWW to drink while the barman is being ridiculously slow to serve the complete order. You also make sure that when other people are buying a round, you ask for a large.

Q. HAVE YOU EVER BEEN POORLY AS A RESULT OF DRINKING TOO MUCH DWW?

a) No, but you once had a funny pork pie at the country fair.
b) You've had a few hangovers in your time but these days you tend to fob them off by being sensible and drinking lots of water.
c) Yes, on more than one occasion you have ended up in A and E with a broken collar bone.

Q. DO PEOPLE SOMETIMES MAKE COMMENTS ABOUT YOUR DRINKING?

a) Yes, they say things like 'Come on you miserable cow, have a drink. It'll liven you up.'
b) No, though a woman once snapped at you for spilling some red wine on her camel coat at a private view.
c) Yes, all the time. That's why you've started doing it in secret.

Q. HAVE YOU EVER DONE ANYTHING SILLY AS A RESULT OF DRINKING TOO MUCH?

a) No, though once you had to scale a wall to use a public convenience because you'd been caught short.
b) You have on occasion danced with maybe too much abandon and shown your bra straps.
c) Yes, you have slept with men who look like they live under a carpet.

WELL, ARE YOU...?

Mostly As

We wonder why you bother to drink at all. You've probably got the one bottle of DWW in the fridge that has lasted you months. Have you discovered some of the wonderful new wine stoppers that keep wine fresh in the fridge for up to a year?

Mostly Bs

To say that you're a social drinker might be understating it since people are notoriously delusional about how much DWW they actually drink. You don't need to worry yet, but some things to look out for might be excessive catalogue ordering, headaches that won't shift, and friends that don't return your calls anymore.

Mostly Cs

Oh dear, this could lead to sherry addiction, which is clearly not the way to go, and has to be tackled as soon as possible. You will need to empty the house of DWW or ask a friend to do so, then sign up for evening classes to fill those dangerous empty evenings. That way you'll be both busy and bored rigid and won't have the time (or money) to waste on the demon DWW.

TRAY GAME™

***M**any people complain about how expensive it is to amuse one's friends and family, but with a little bit of imagination you can have all sorts of fun in the home without spending a single penny.*

Here at *Wendy* we are big fans of Fun on a Budget so why not roll back the hands of time and enjoy yourself like we used to in the days before colour television and drinking alcohol in the middle of the week for no reason whatsoever.

The Tray Game™ is a family favourite that is in danger of being forgotten. We used to play this at parties back in the sixties when parents understood that letting children have too much fun was dangerous, especially straight after a rich and sugary party tea. But The Tray Game™ needn't be relegated to children's parties. Why not play the game with your adult friends? Place twenty items on a tray and let everyone stare at these items for a minute. Then cover the tray with a tea towel and now see who can remember the most items. If any of your friends consistently score low marks, you should maybe get them to have a nice chat with their GP.

Some suggested items for The Tray Game™

A BIRO
SOME NAIL SCISSORS
A TUNING FORK
A DARNING MUSHROOM
A PEBBLE
A TILL RECEIPT
A SMALL TUBE OF OINTMENT
A CORK
A NAIL FILE
A POUND COIN
(KEEP YOUR EYE ON THIS)

A RUBBER BAND OR HAIR BOBBLE
A LIGHTER/BOX OF MATCHES
A LIPSTICK OR MASCARA WAND
AN EGG CUP
A SHOE LACE
A BATTERY
A COTTON REEL
A WAX CRAYON
A TOY CAR
AN ASPIRIN

THIS GAME SUCKS. WISH WE WERE PLAYING THE TRAY GAME™

Obviously only use items that are lying around the house. If you do not own some of the suggestions on our list, do not go out and buy them, use your imagination or ask someone with an imagination to help.

FOR THE BOARD GAME ENTHUSIASTS AMONGST YOU. HERE ARE SOME IDEAS OF WHAT TO USE WHEN YOU HAVE LOST YOUR CLUEDO IMPLEMENTS OR YOUR MONOPOLY PIECES.
PAPER CLIPS, PEN LIDS, BUTTONS, FALSE NAILS, A SMALL EYE SHADOW, A WALNUT (OR ANY NUT IN A SHELL), A KEY, THE RING PULL FROM A CAN OF DRINK, A MINIATURE PLASTIC SOLDIER, A PIECE OF LEGO, AN OPAL FRUIT.

WENDY SAYS

* There are lots of battery operated brain-training games around at the moment. We would just like to say that here at *Wendy* we think The Tray Game™ is the original and best.

THE HOBBY HABIT

In your youth your hobbies were drinking, getting off with boys and dyeing your hair, but now that you're (apparently) a respectable middle-aged women, you need to move on to something more appropriate to your age group. You'll need a hobby that will get you out of the house (very important now) and keep your hands busy when they might otherwise be in the biscuit tin.

But have you thought about the medical implications of some of the hobbies you may be toying with? Our resident medical expert, Dr Rudolf Clerc, has his say on the pros and cons of some of our most popular hobbies.

Knitting

Dr Rudolf Clerc: Knitting should only be practised by women who can be trusted with sharp implements. Perhaps a full mental health assessment should be made before purchasing needles. For the older lady, already prone to arthritis or rheumatism, it might be best to reserve knitting just for summer when one's joint conditions are less severe.

Occasionally women will suffer a condition known to the profession as 'knitting frenzy'- when the sufferer can't stop knitting and somehow loses the ability to cast off. If this happens it's best to approach the victim very carefully and gently remove the needles and wool from her hands, zip said items firmly away into a knitting bag, and tell her that on no account is she allowed to knit for at least 24 hours.

Jigsaws

Dr Rudolf Clerc: In my professional opinion, jigsaws are entirely safe. There's no need for a visit to your GP before embarking on this hobby. However, if you have very high blood pressure, it's best not to buy your puzzles from car boot sales as sometimes several pieces are missing: this might aggravate you into having a nasty turn.

Don't expect your jigsaw to be easily transported. If you want a portable jigsaw you are going to have to invest in some specialist equipment. By the same token, beware doing the jigsaw on the dining-room table. You might need to clear it at a crucial moment, which could lead to emotional upset and resentment.

Picking on shop girls

Dr Rudolf Clerc: picking on shop girls is an attractive pastime for women of a certain age, and there are some distinct health benefits from being able to let off consumer rage in this way. It's the gratis equivalent of primal scream therapy – in fact, in many ways it is primal screaming. However, you do have to be aware of the possible drawbacks. Shop girls are devious and may stage retaliation by leaving a security tag on and getting you arrested, or taking down your credit card details and flogging them on eBay for identity fraud.

Learn a foreign language

Dr Rudolf Clerc: On the face of it, learning a foreign language is one of the safest hobbies anyone of any age might choose to take up. That said, there a couple of precautions one must take: beware the foreign language disc in the car, as it's easy to lose concentration when one is sorting one's masculine pronouns from the feminine. And on a more emotional level, take care not to alienate loved ones. Just because you can suddenly count to a million in French doesn't mean they necessarily want to listen to you demonstrate this skill.

There is also some evidence to suggest that vulnerable middle-aged women, especially the recently separated or divorced, can find themselves inappropriately attached to their language teachers, even more so if these teachers are around thirty with slim hips and nice eyes.

Writing to the council

Dr Rudolf Clerc: I can honestly say that, from a medical perspective, this is without a doubt the most dangerous pastime for women of a certain age. Nothing is more likely to raise your blood pressure or bring on a stroke than writing to or trying to call the council. Plus, make too much of a nuisance of yourself and the dustbin men will accidentally on purpose forget to empty your bin and you will have to decant the contents and put it in bin bags and put it in your car and take it all to the tip until your turn comes around again. You will never beat them. Never.

Juggling

Dr Rudolf Clerc: I would not advise many women over forty to take up juggling. It's unattractive at any age but for those of mature years, it's a positive health hazard. For example, women have been known to concentrate so hard on catching the balls or bean bags that they've forgotten to look where they're going, which has further resulted in tumbling off pavements into traffic, skidding in dog faeces, accidentally falling backwards into boating lakes and all sorts of other potentially lethal situations.

The bigger-breasted female will find herself at a juggling disadvantage compared to her flatter-chested sister – a serious practical issue to take into consideration if you are thinking about taking up this most dangerous of armchair activities.

Lolling

(derived from the latin 'Lolloxificius' – meaning to lounge in a supine manner at any opportune moment)

Dr Rudolf Clerc: Lolling for the uninitiated involves some form of inertia – normally lying down on a sofa or in a bath, with a glass of dry white wine and intellectually unchallenging reading material. Crucially, lolling has to be performed when everyone else is out of the house. If other members of the family see you lolling, they will assume you don't have enough to do or don't have as much to do as you are always saying you have, and give you some Little Jobs to do.

Prolonged lolling can be dangerous for those with low blood pressure – sudden movement after being inert for so long may bring on dizziness or balance problems, so getting up off the sofa every hour may be a sensible precaution. Annoying we know, but you can't be too careful.

Drinking while lolling can set you off on a slippery slope. Many start innocently enough with a cup of tea, but soon graduate to a glass of white wine to compliment their *Heat* magazine, book, or brain trainer Nintendo. Know the danger signs would be my advice – for instance lolling with a dry white wine on a Friday night at 7.30 is fine, but taking the day off work to loll on your sofa all day with a bottle is a definite sign of hard lolling and something to be taken very seriously indeed.

Finding out about your family tree

Dr Rudolf Clerc: Beware any activity that can turn you from an averagely popular person into a complete and utter hobby bore. This is one. The main thing to remember when exploring your family tree is that it's *your* family and of very little interest to anyone else. Be careful too of what you dig up as there might be some pretty rotten branches on that tree. Can you really cope with the fact that your great-great-great-grandfather was the local flasher and that most of your ancestors died of syphilis?

ARE YOU SUFFERING FROM
EMPTY NEST SYNDROME?

GOODBYE TO ALL THAT

As all mums know, having children is not easy. First of all they ruin your womb and breasts, then they wreck your nice tidy home and finally they destroy your piece of mind, leaving you gibbering about UCAS forms and looking up signs of 'drug abuse' on the internet.

Why we bother having them in the first place is an absolute mystery. If most of us knew how ungrateful the mewling, puking things we once held so lovingly in our arms were going to be, then many of us would have had our tubes tied at puberty.

The irony is, it's just when you have started to treat each other as human beings, having overcome the bilious rage of the teenager, that it's time for your child to fly the nest. You have dragged your offspring from birth to adulthood and the final proof that your job is done is when they can no longer bare to live under the same roof as you. The gratitude! And it's all your fault.

If they're going to university, it's your fault for being academically pushy. If they're going travelling, it's your fault for making them stand on their own two feet, if they're just buggering off to cotch on a sofa at a mate's house, it's your fault for not being pushy enough.

There are different ways of coping with the empty nest: some women find that a hobby or a dog tide them over, others can't wait to see the back of their kids, others don't even notice they've gone. So, what kind of empty nest mum are you?

Take this quick quiz and find out whether you're going to be celebrating seeing the back of them with a cruise around the Greek islands or whether you're more likely to be sobbing on the bed taking great handfuls of anti-depressants.

ANSWERS

Mostly As: No wonder your kids couldn't wait to leave home, they needed to get away from you breathing down their necks and meddling with their lives. Get a grip, or failing that, get a hobby.

Mostly Bs: No wonder your kids couldn't wait to leave home. What sort of a mother are you? A selfish and uncaring one, that's what.

See, you can't win.

The Empty Nest Quiz

Now that they've left home and you find yourself in the supermarket, do you…
A) Buy loads of food which goes off in the fridge because you have forgotten that there are no longer three teenagers and their mates eating you out of house and home?

B) Not bother? These days you eat out all the time; now those gannets have gone you can afford lovely swish meals in posh restaurants.

Now that the house is empty do you…
A) Wander into your children's empty bedrooms and sniff their dressing gowns?

B) Let their rooms to some nice young men?

With time on your hands do you…
A) Dig out albums of old photos, look at pictures of old family holidays and cry?

B) Have a nice manicure?

When you're out and about do you…
A) Look hungrily at women in the park with young children and pull faces to make the toddler laugh?

B) Avoid places where there might be small children making a silly noise and mess? Thank God you don't have to feed those tedious ducks ever again.

When you're off on a drive do you…
A) Keep looking round to see if everyone is in the car when actually there's just you, him and the radio?

B) Think how fantastic it is to have traded that dreary Volvo for your sexy new two-seater Porsche?

At tea time do you…
A) Really miss finishing off their unwanted fish fingers?

B) Have a nice gin and tonic?

Do you spend your evenings…
A) Looking up adopting orphans on the internet?

B) Salsa dancing?

Have you put on weight since they left?
A) Yes, because you finish the ironing before Coronation Street is over and start eating biscuits because you don't know what else to do with your hands.

B) No, you've spent their inheritance on liposuction. Hoorah!

AND THEY CALL IT BUDGIE LOVE

Joan had been married to Ken Pennington for thirty years. Theirs was a loving relationship, with a few arguments over Ken's miniature railway – and Joan's peculiar crush on Nigel Havers – but all in all they rubbed along quite nicely.

The Penningtons had two children who had long since grown up and moved away, Suzie to Leamington Spa and Glenn all the way to Brisbane in Australia. In fact, the Penningtons were saving up for a 'Trip of a Lifetime' when Ken didn't come down for his lunch one Saturday.

He'll be messing about with that wretched railways set, fumed Joan. She'd made a lovely leek and potato soup and it was now getting cold on the kitchen table.

But it wasn't just the soup that was getting cold. By the time she climbed the ladder to the attic, Ken Pennington was chilly to the touch.

'A massive stroke,' the coroner said, 'at least he didn't suffer.'

No, Ken wasn't suffering; it was Joan who was in pieces. I'm lonely, she admitted to herself.

After Ken had been gone for three months, and all the shock and fuss over his funeral had calmed down, Joan thought, I should start pulling myself together, but it was hard and sometimes she found herself still setting the table for two.

'You could do with a pet,' her daughter said. Suzie was very practical.

'I don't want anything that involves too much looking after,' said Joan. 'I'm allergic to cats and I'm scared of dogs.'

'What about a tortoise?' asked Suzie.

'Don't be daft,' her mother replied. 'You can't love a tortoise.'

Joan put an advert in the local paper: miniature railway for sale. A very nice man came round; he wanted to buy it for his grandson.

'My granddaughters aren't interested,' sighed Joan, 'and the only grandson I've got lives on the other side of the world.'

'Have you ever thought about a budgie?' asked Brian. Brian Perkins was sixty-three, a nice-looking man with a good head of hair. 'Only I breed them, just a hobby, since my wife died and well…'

Three weeks later Brian was back. He brought a cage, complete with a perch, some Trill and a swing – but that wasn't all he brought with him.

'I'm going to call her Carmen,' said Joan, 'because she's so colourful, like Carmen Miranda.'

'Ring me if you've got any problems,' said Brian. 'In fact, I'll call you in a couple of days to see how you're getting on.'

When Brian phoned three days later Joan wasn't feeling too good. I've got a dreadful headache, she thought to herself.

'How's Carmen?' asked Brian.

'Well,' said Joan, 'she's off her trill and she seems to be sleeping all the time.'

'That sounds odd,' said Brian. 'Listen, Joan, I'm a bit worried. I'll coming over.'

It took Brian forty minutes to drive to Joan's. He drove as fast as he could. Something wasn't right; he could feel it in his bones.

Joan didn't answer when he rang the bell. Brian wrapped his sweater round his hand and broke the glass in the front door. Reaching round for the latch he let himself into the house.

'…she's off her trill and she seems to be sleeping all the time.'

It was too late to save Carmen. She was lying on the floor of her cage. She wasn't breathing and Brian knew there was no chance of saving her – but what about Joan?

Joan lay slumped in her chair. Without pausing Brian scooped her into his arms and rushed her out of the house. She was still alive and to Brian's relief the ambulance turned up within minutes.

'It was the gas fire,' whispered Joan the next day. 'It was leaking. I could have been killed – thank you.'

'It's all right,' said Brian. 'It's just when you said Carmen wasn't well, alarm bells went off in my head.'

'Poor Carmen,' whispered Joan, and a tear slid down her cheek.

'Don't worry, Joan,' said Brian. 'I can always get you another budgie and if you don't want another budgie, you can always have me.'

Brian reached for Joan's hand and weak as she was, Joan squeezed it. 'That would be nice,' she smiled.

THE END

THE TOO LATE TO LEARN CENTRE presents...

The NOKIA Bog Standard

Fed up of fancy phones? Added features driving you wild? Then this revolutionary mobile phone is the answer. Simply put, this miraculous gadget lets you make and receive phone calls, and nothing else!

Yours for £11.99

No hidden extras guaranteed: No camera, no WAP, no emails, no video, no fancy ring tones or wallpapers, no time and date settings. Its the new, improved, just-a-phone phone. Wind up mechanism for recharging.

FOR THE WOMEN WITH A SNORING MAN COME...

PILLOW MUFFS!

An ingenious solution to those sleepless nights. Also perfect for a chilly day or a walk on the beach to keep the wind out of your ears.

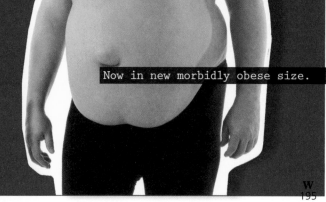

LOSE 3 STONE OVERNIGHT!

Just buy one of our fantastic Fat n' Ugly cardboard cut outs, place in passenger seat or on bar stool next to you and instantly feel sexier, slimmer, and more confident in a jiffy.

Now in new morbidly obese size.

THE RIGHT DOG FOR YOU

Although a dog is supposed to be 'Man's best friend', there's no reason why a woman can't have a doggie chum too. In fact, let's face it, whenever there's a pet in the family, who is it that ends up taking it for walks and making sure it has its jabs? It's us, that's who!

BUT EVEN IF YOU DON'T LIKE DOGS THERE COMES A TIME WHEN YOU HAVE TO BUY ONE AND HERE ARE TEN GOOD REASONS FOR CAVING IN TO THE DOG OWNER THING.

1. You are suffering from empty nest syndrome

2. You don't want to be the only thing asleep in front of the fire farting

3. You need something that will give you love without expecting sex

4. If you don't have something to take out for a walk, you will end up dead and having to be winched out of your house

5. You daren't get a cat in case the local children think you really are a witch

6. You like throwing old tennis balls

7. Having your faced licked is not something that fills you with repulsion. Any kind of affection is OK these days

8. Maybe you will meet a handsome widower whilst you are out dog walking

9. You are physically unable to have another baby and too scared to adopt or steal one. What other choice do you really have?

10. Hamsters are nocturnal, smell and eat their young, terrapins have got horrible eyes, and budgies won't shut up. Lets face it, it's got to be a dog

So, now you've accepted the inevitable, what's the dog for you? Here's a handy little quiz, lovingly put together by us kind people here at *Wendy*, to lead you to your perfect new best friend.

Would you keep your dog…
A) Outside in the yard on a thick metal chain?
B) In your handbag?
C) In a dog basket in the kitchen next to the Aga?
D) On your bed, even though it's not meant to be?

Would you call it…
A) Satan?
B) Ninnypoo?
C) Honey?
D) Piggy (because it has a curly tail)?

Would you buy your dog from…
A) A man in the pub?
B) A breeder who sold a very similar dog to Geri Halliwell?
C) A dear old stick in Tiverton?
D) Battersea Dogs' Home?

Would you feed it…
A) People's ankles?
B) Minced chicken?
C) Pedigree Chum?
D) Chocolate biscuits?

HOW DID YOU SCORE?

Mostly As: You're the sort of person that shouldn't be allowed children, never mind dogs. No doubt you want one of those killing machines like a Pit Bull or a Rottweiler. Oh well, as long as you don't live near us.

Mostly Bs: You don't really want a dog because you're actually scared of them and you're just trying to be fashionable. You'll probably end up paying way over the odds for one of those stupid Shitzu things or a Chihuahua which will probably die from catching a cold or getting trapped in the hoover.

Mostly Cs: Congratulations, you are ideal dog-owning material, treat yourself to a nice pedigree Labrador and we promise you years of loyalty and happiness which may go some way to making up for the other things that have gone wrong in your life.

Mostly Ds: Considering you're a bit doggy yourself, we think you'd be best off with a fun-loving mongrel. Your house is probably too grubby for paw prints to matter, so just make sure you keep your cereal bowls and the dog bowl separate. There's casual and then there's slovenly.

TIP: Remember dogging is something very odd people do in car parks and has nothing whatsoever to do with normal people and their pets

THRIFT

Now that no one has a job for life anymore and there's no such thing as a safe pension plan, most of us need to start tightening our belts if we're not going to spend our twilight years eating tinned cat food! From braising a piece of brisket (four days on a low light) to turning a plate of rhubarb crumble into a draft excluder (all you need is a pair of tights, a hair dryer and some air freshener) here are some fun penny-pinching ideas to keep even the most miserly happy.

Regifting

Why not repossess all those presents you have given demented loved ones and wrap them up again for forthcoming birthdays/Mother's Days/Christmases. They will be none the wiser and if they liked it the first time chances are they'll like it second time around too.

Stinky Drawers?

For an alternative to the lavender bag, why not place one of those urinal cakes* in a child's sock, sew the open end of the sock together and, hey presto, an instant drawer freshener.

*WARNING: urinal cakes are not edible, they are solid chemical air-fresheners commonly seen in men's urinals. Do not eat them, no matter how hungry you are.

Waste Not Want Not

Saving random items is a great hobby for women who don't really know what to do with themselves. Start by collecting some polystyrene trays – just the idea that you are saving something that you would otherwise have thrown away will give you a deep glow of satisfaction. Once you've saved about 7,000 trays, you can soundproof the spare bedroom, which is a boon when you have fornicating friends to stay (Hoorah! No more lying there listening to their carnal grunting). Alternatively they could be painted and varnished and used as attractive gift presentation platters for those more difficult to regift unwanted photo frames and necklace and earring sets you've got stored in the spare wardrobe.

Darning is the New Rock and Roll

Got a cardi that's gone through at the elbow, why not pop a patch on it? The great thing about darning is that anyone with suede elbow patches looks like a batty old professor, even if you haven't got a single O level. Best worn with bifocals to complete the Oxbridge Don look.

Christmas is a Nightmare for the Thrift Conscious...

So why not suggest that this Christmas becomes a Charity Shop Christmas? Instead of spending a hideous amount of money on new presents for your loved ones, make a deal with everyone that only gifts bought in charity shops are acceptable. Your money will be going to a good cause and you'll also be cutting down on your carbon footprint. Which is marvellous. Well, it's marvellous until Christmas morning and you all open smelly old second-hand bric-a-brac and nasty towelling dressing gowns... Obviously, if you have family members who are prone to suicide attempts or manic depression this may just send them over the edge (which, with this being Christmas, they were teetering on the brink of anyway). Worth bearing in mind.

Make Your Own Jewellery

Spray macaroni gold and thread on some red ribbon for a really fun festive necklace.

NB Do not attempt to boil the macaroni after it has been sprayed gold, as the spray paint might contain carcinogenics.

Why Not Make Your Own Mosaics?

The thrifty alternative to buying expensive tranquillisers on the internet
Feeling furious? Why not smash a load of old china up against your back wall (assorted patterned plates and saucers work best), gather up the fragments and make an attractive mosaic.

Things you can mosaic:
An old vase
A picture frame
The shower room (this is quite a big job so ideal if you have lots of anger issues)

Why Waste Those Empty Loo Rolls?

Fill them with cotton wool and thread with string to make your own tampons (for those very heavy days). Cheap and environmentally friendly too.

Use Your Imagination

Got an old toothbrush that's past its best? Why not use it for cleaning the inside of the loo. Do be careful not to get it mixed up with family toothbrushes still in circulation, unless the old man is really, really annoying you. 'Oh gosh silly me.'

A SPECIAL ON CUSTOMER SERVICES

Taking things back is one of those chores that traditionally falls on women's shoulders, since no one else in the family can be arsed to find the right bag, the right receipt and the right excuse and then stand in a queue for an entire lunch hour. To get the most out of the customer services desk, it's best to see taking something back not as the time-consuming hassle it is, but rather as sport, a challenge to your skills as woman. Below are some tried and tested techniques and tips for getting one over the shop assistant and putting the victory back into the everyday.

❧ THE NO RECEIPT SCENARIO ❧

You've got home, changed your mind, lost the receipt…

1. Take it back in the right bag. It's no good taking something back in a WHSmiths bag to Primark, it just screams out I've already worn it/soiled it/washed it.
2. Wear something smart. Ideally a coat with a brooch on, and a handbag that you hold at the wrist like the Queen.
3. Smile scarily.
4. Put on your poshest accent.
5. Put a coat hanger in the bag. They'll think you've barely taken it out of the bag and that the receipt wasn't put in the bag in the first place.
6. Hold your nerve.
7. Pace yourself. It's no good demanding to see the manager when all she's asked so far is 'When did you buy it?'
8. Once you've told her that you don't have the receipt you'll need to blather on with some small talk. Whatever you do keep talking, because she'll be inspecting it for signs of wear and tear.
9. If she goes behind the screen, she's gone to find the supervisor. This is a bad sign. You will need to prepare a 'Gosh! Silly me' speech to retain dignity.
10. Alternatively, try the fall back position – a credit note. As long as the items don't smell (too much) or you still have the box, you might be in with a chance.
11. Once you've got your full refund or credit note do not do a victory lap round the queue, however tempting. It will make taking things back next time all the more difficult.

❧ ADVANCED TAKING BACK ❧

You've worn it, or used it just the once…

1. Wear a hat. The more formal the better
2. Iron or clean the item in question. Remember, iron on the inside – a shiny jumper is a dead give away.
3. Ideally keep the labels of everything you buy, or just never take them off. Get into the habit of wearing the label tucked in. It will give you a big advantage when you get to the supervisor situation at customer services.
4. Once she's gone through the ritual of inspecting the garment for signs of wear and tear, you may need to feign illness or dizziness. Alternatively, blather on about the shirt, saying it looked nice but didn't really go with the outfit you had in mind, anything to take her mind off the fact that it is looking ragged and limp.
5. If the supervisor appears in person from behind the screen, brace yourself for a potential punch up; especially if she is holding your garment at arm's length and turning up her nose at the obvious smell. Your only course of action is to feign astonishment. It's your word against hers. Go very la di da and tell her she's calling your integrity into question. With any luck she'll be so scared she'll give in. Or she'll manfully stand her ground and you will have to walk away, head hung low.

Wendy's Short Stories

 MEETING PAUL

Looking back, I couldn't blame them for being worried. My daughters are good girls and they didn't want me to be lonely. I tried telling them I wasn't but they didn't believe me and maybe deep down, it wasn't true. But then I met Paul. The day Paul came into my life everyone was happy.

The girls were thrilled because at last I was getting out and about, seeing films, going out for dinner.

They were also a bit relieved. Neither of them live that close by and if I visit them I have to stay and sometimes that's not terribly convenient. Don't get me wrong, I enjoy visiting my girls, but the grandchildren are getting to that answering back and being rude stage and sometimes I find the whoe thing quite stressful, and, between you and me, I can't stand Caroline's husband!

So meeting Paul was a real blessing. At last, I had someone to spend my weekends with and the girls didn't have to feel so guilty about me rattling around the house on my own.

I blame their father, of course, for the guilt thing.

The girls were very upset when their father and I got divorced. They were even more upset when he disappeared off to Australia with his new young wife and started another family somewhere near Manley Beach, which I believe is near Sydney (not that I've looked it up on the internet or anything). They were upset that their father had decided to put a line under one life and embark upon another, leaving yours truly a bit redundant.

Because that's the truth of it, when your duties as wife and mother are no longer needed, women like me can feel a bit, well, surplus to requirements. But you do get used to it and after a while, I realised there were pros to being on your own. I could do what I like when I liked – but that wasn't good enough for the girls.

'Mum, you need to meet more people. You don't want to be stuck in on your own. You're still an attractive woman, why don't you join a club?'

So, I did, I joined a sports club and I played tennis every Friday evening, swam on Saturday mornings and did a Pilates class on Sunday afternoons.

'You've not lost much weight,' said Caroline when I last visited. 'I'd have thought with all that sport you'd be wasting away.'

'Yes, well,' I said, 'I seem to have found my appetite for other things.'

It was Caroline's husband's big old smirky face that made me do it.

'I see,' he smarmed, 'so you've re-found your appetite, your *joie de vivre*, and would he have a name?'

I didn't mean to but I couldn't help it. 'Paul,' I said. 'His name is Paul. We've only just met and it's nothing serious but he's very nice.'

After that I was bombarded. When I got back from Caroline's, my other daughter Edwina was on the

phone before I'd got in the door. 'So what's he like, this Paul?'

I was cornered. I told her that the relationship was very new and it was none of her business, but she just went on, so I told her how he was in his early sixties and did something to do with importing wine and that he travelled a lot and was very keen on sailing.

'So he's posh,' trilled Edwina and I found myself agreeing, 'Yes, he's sort of posh.'

'So he's posh...'

'Well,' she said, 'you can tell me more about him when you next come up for the weekend. How about next Saturday?'

I thought about it and deep down I didn't want to go. Edwina has three boys who smell and shout and fight and fart. Lunch with them is enough; a weekend is some kind of punishment.

'I'm sorry,' I told her. 'I'm going to the Norfolk Broads with Paul.'

Twenty minutes later Caroline called me and gave me a long lecture about safe sex and the over-sixties. I couldn't help it, I sniggered. She was shocked, which was good. Caroline can be a little priggish. It's her husband's fault: Glenn is a dreadful snob.

'We're staying at The Bell,' I boasted, knowing that would impress snobby Glenn.

Being with Paul was marvellous. The first six months of our relationship were a whirl, when we weren't playing tennis or hopping over to Paris for the weekend, then we were visiting art galleries and watching movies. I was really busy, I barely had time to speak to the girls, never mind visit.

I bought new clothes, shoes and spent more money on a bag than my first honeymoon had cost. I was very happy indeed, Paul made me happy, all six foot two of him.

'What does he look like?'

asked Edwina, when she phoned one night.

'A bit like Michael Aspel, but tall,' I replied.

Of course, as time went on I had to answer more and more questions.

'Was he married?'

Had been but not anymore.

'Any children?'

One son, lives in the Loire Valley, in the wine trade like his dad.

'What does he drive?'

A Mercedes.

'What sort of Mercedes?'

A silver one.

Fortunately at this point, just when the grilling was getting a bit much, Paul rang the doorbell. 'I've got to go, it's Paul. We're going salsa dancing.'

I knew that eventually, they'd want to meet him. But, as I said to Caroline, I didn't need her permission to go out with a man, I am an adult. I'm nearly…

She finished the sentence. 'Sixty, and that's why we've arranged a birthday lunch.'

'Where?' I stuttered.

'Well, you had such a great time at The Bell – we thought we'd book us all in there.'

'But it's far too far to drive,' I protested.

'Yes,' she agreed. 'But it's half term so we can stay the night and drive back the next day. Anyway, you can't argue, it's all sorted.'

All of us were invited, me and Glenn, Charlie (my eldest grandson, an odd boy takes after his father), Edwina, Phil (Edwina's husband), their three boys and, of course, Paul.

The silly thing is, I bought a new dress. a navy silk Diane von Furstenberg wraparound and red patent shoes – I knew exactly what Paul liked me in.

I drove myself up to Norfolk. I wore the dress and changed into the shoes when I reached the hotel. Just before I entered the dining room I took a deep breath. They were all there, my daughters, their husbands, their children.

'Happy Birthday!' they cheered and a waiter cracked open a bottle of champagne. There were two empty chairs at the top of the table. I sat down in one of them.

There was a small silence. 'So, where is the famous Paul?' asked smarmy Glenn.

I had a choice then. I could have made something else up, I could have said we'd been involved in an accident on the way and he'd been killed, but I couldn't lie anymore: I told the truth.

I said, 'Paul doesn't exist; I made him up. For the last six months I have been having the most fantastic relationship with an imaginary boyfriend and may I just say that the conversation has been scintillating and the sex out of this world!'

The silence stretched, then Josh, Edwina's middle boy, whistled, 'Whoa, cool, Grandma.'

And I couldn't help it, I laughed.

THE END

HOW DOES YOUR GARDEN GROW?

POISON IVAN, STYLE ICON, TOTALITARIAN SYMPATHISER AND AMATEUR HORTICULTURIST, GETS HIS GREEN FINGERS DIRTY WITH YOUR CHOICE OF GARDEN DESIGN

THE ROMANTIC GARDEN

The trouble with you is that you want life to be one great big bowl of cherries. Thing is, sweetheart, under every strawberry patch there's usually one enormous great slug! First things first, make sure that slug isn't the man in your life. For starters, make sure he's not leaving a sticky white slimy trail all over your sofa cushions and when he's out of the room check his phone and find out whether he's texting other women. Just because you're a nice, sweet, old-fashioned kind of girl doesn't mean to say that he's not a two-timing rat. In fact, it's probably because you are such an airy-fairy, silly old cow that he's taking you for a complete ride – I'd check your savings account if I were you.

Your problem is that you see life through rose-tinted spectacles, but tend to forget that you can't make a rainbow without a bit of rain. Just make sure you're ready for a downpour, girl, it'll probably come when you're least expecting it and just when you've had your hair done.

THE PRACTICAL GARDEN

On the one hand, this is the ideal garden: minimal lawn mowing, no weeding – which means no lumbago – and all your stinking household waste mulching away nicely in the corner, but what's the point in making compost if you haven't got any roses? Judging by your pants – those great big monstrosities that are hanging up to dry – you've crossed the line from sensible to dull and need to get some colour back into your life. People think they can rely on you, which is just another way of saying people think they can take advantage of you. You're so busy running round doing those tedious little jobs that no one else can be arsed to do, that you've no time for yourself, which is probably why you haven't noticed that your legs need shaving and you're wearing a really horrible skirt. Have a good look at yourself. Are you as plain as your back garden? Is your husband spending a lot of time standing at the window in the spare room looking at the woman next door who is sunbathing with her top off? Go mad – invest in some geraniums, get a rinse put in your hair, buy some yellow sandals, brighten yourself and the garden up, get a sun lounger out, take <u>your</u> top off, and if he's still looking over the garden fence after all that, no easy way to say it: you're in trouble.

NEW AGE

Well, well Miss Patchouli 1976, where have we been? In some fashion coma for the last thirty-odd years? Wake up, take down the Che Guevara posters and smell the scented candles. No one's doing joss sticks anymore, mung beans are out, and minimalist chic is in. You're so far behind you might never find your way into the 21st century. You call yourself a healer but the only reason why people tell you that your 'magical' hands have worked is because they don't want you touching them for another second longer. Oh yes, and that Dandelion wine you gave everyone for Christmas, they call it, 'The Drain Cleaner'. As for the hair, the henna has to go – change it for a nice bob. Face it, love, you're getting a bit matted at the back.

THE SLOB

So common it hurts. You probably smoke indoors, don't you? All over those poor defenceless grandkiddies who will all have asthma and learning difficulties and are called things like Britnee and Kaylee and Leeyum. Judging by the mounds of dog poo, you don't believe in scooping, not even if it's on the carpet. You're not interested in fresh air or horticulture, in fact you probably don't know what horticulture means. I'd tell you go and look it up, but you probably don't have a dictionary in your house. All I can say is I'm glad I don't live next door to your horrible barking dog and screaming kids. I bet you're living on benefits and you've probably got tattoos on your face. Your friends don't really like you, you know? They're just scared of you.

Wendy's Jobs For Girls

What the stars say about your work life

Capricorn

THE HARD-WORKING DUTIFUL GOAT

There's nothing a Capricorn likes more than feeling morally superior, so why not take a job teaching in a run-down secondary modern? It might not pay much, but at least you can bang on about having principles in the pub (over half a lager, which is all you'll be able to afford). Considering that you get off on being right, it makes sense to choose a profession in which you're likely to be better educated than the people you are working with, like stupid kids, inept idiots or ridiculous felons.

Capricorn is one of the least sympathetic of the star signs, so you're not likely to be taken in by the stupid 'My dog died so I couldn't do my homework' or 'I had a bad time as a kiddie' excuses. Some people might call you a hard-hearted old bitch behind your back – and yes, you are – but it's like you say 'At least you're not a sponge on society'.

Wendy suggests:
SOCIAL WORKER
TEACHER
PROBATION OFFICER/PRISON OFFICER

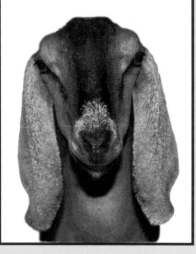

Devil's work

Aquarius

THE WATER CARRIER AKA, THE CLEANER

Despite being unsentimental to the point of social awkwardness, Aquarians are the do-gooders of the zodiac. Traditionally, being water carriers, they were also the purifiers of the zodiac, which these days translates into a mop and slop bucket.

Considering their passion for hygiene, many Aquarians make great cleaners – in fact, in a recent survey we conducted, Aquarians came second only to the Filipinos in a league table of best home helps.

For the ambitious Aquarian, cleanliness isn't the only thing next to godliness, there's nursing too! Aquarians aren't known for their squeamishness and there's nothing they enjoy more than cleaning up blood, sick and poo.

Of course, not every single one wants to work either as a cleaner or a nurse, so for those who lack people skills and are devoid of any human emotion whatseover, why not be a traffic warden?

Wendy suggests:
NURSE
CLEANER/CARE WORKER
TRAFFIC WARDEN

Pisces

THE THIRSTY FISH

Pisceans are socially the most hopeless of all the star signs, which doesn't for a second mean to say they don't like a good party. If anything, parties are their weakness – they can't stop partying for long enough to do anything useful. Pisceans are easily led and find it difficult to say no (to another drink mostly), they are also terrible show offs and want to be the centre of attention at all times. Most Pisceans crave fame regardless of whether or not they have any talent, which they usually don't.

Many of the world's worst actresses and actors are Pisceans, and you know what they say, 'If you can't beat them, join them'. There's a latent Am Dram star in you yet! It's been said that many Pisceans think they are undiscovered geniuses, but most of them are actually just idiots.

Wendy suggests:
POET
DRUNK
ACTOR

We all know that the position of the stars and planets have a great deal to do with our love lives, but what about our work lives? Exhaustive research from Wendy's in-house team of crack astrologers has shown that a successful career often depends on the right star sign being in the right job. News to us too. So, if you're feeling like you're not really getting anywhere, if those promotions keep going to the silly cow who sits next to you, if you wake up everyday feeling unfulfilled and furious at the prospect of spending yet another day flogging your guts out for 'those idiots', chances are you could be in the wrong job. Yes, you could be a Pisces doing something that would suit a Capricorn much better (Pisceans can't file. Neither can Capricorns, but at least they'll try).

REMEMBER – Finding the right job to suit you isn't just about having the correct qualifications and experience, it's sometimes about nepotism too, but every now and again it's about destiny…

Aries

THE BRAVE IF FOOLHARDY RAM

Of all the star signs, Aries are the bravest, most suited to life outdoors and are the least fussed about make-up, all of which points to a career in the military, because, let's face it, you can't be fussing with your hair when you're under enemy crossfire in downtown Basra.

Aries, regardless of whether they're men or women (to be honest they're both equally butch) are physically stronger than most of the other star signs which is why they tend to do a lot of arm wrestling for fun. Not being blessed with much of an imagination, Arians make good police constables but very few of them make it to special branch.

They are good at stuff like tying knots and saving drowning kids, which makes them ideal camp leaders on outward bound courses. Female Arians tend not to complain about things like periods or PMT or PMS or the menapause, which makes them popular with male employers, and lesbians.

Wendy suggests:
POLICE
ARMY
ADVENTURE LEADER/PIONEER

Taurus

THE TRUSTWORTHY (NO) BULL (SHI**ER)

The great thing about a Taurean is if you lend her fifty quid, you've got a good chance of getting it back. Taureans are reliable and honest which makes them ideal candidates for the banking profession – unlike everyone else, they simply aren't tempted to stick a fifty-quid note down the front of their blouse.

They're also big fans of mindless routine so waking up at 4.30am to open their stationery shop at 5.30am everyday, for ever and ever, is no hardship for them; in fact they sort of get off on it. That said, your average Taurean has a fearsome temper and a penchant for corporal punishment, so woe betide your casual shoplifter trying to half inch a rolodex. Although they don't like to admit it, Taureans are secretly quite greedy and they like their nosh, which is why many of them find their calling in the kitchen and as a result have the highest cholesterol, and biggest waistlines, of all the star signs.

Wendy suggests:
BANK MANAGER
SHOP KEEPER
COOK

Gemini

THE TALKATIVE TWIN

The thing about Geminis is that they don't half like the sound of their own voice – a trait which might make a job on QVC ideal. They are also very fond of material posessions and can't be trusted not to 'borrow' yours without asking, and so shouldn't be employed anywhere full of unguarded possessions where temptation might strike; rules out the old-people's home. Shame. That said, they are very outgoing and gregarious, in other words not that bright, and so the travel industry could beckon. As the female Gemini is not averse to spending hours in front of the mirror applying luminous orange foundation, air hostessing is a natural employment solution. The other great thing about Gemini women is that they can stand for hours on end without their legs puffing up, so if all else fails, there's always sales.

Wendy suggests:
TV WEATHER GIRL
NATIONAL TRUST GUIDE
HOLIDAY REP

Wendy's Jobs For Girls

★ JOBS TO SUIT YOUR STAR SIGN ★

Cancer

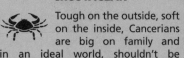

THE SOFT-CENTRED CRUSTACEAN

Tough on the outside, soft on the inside, Cancerians are big on family and in an ideal world, shouldn't be allowed near an office. A Cancerian woman's natural role in life is that of Matriarch, the sort of woman you see on *EastEnders* defending her ghastly relatives because they're 'Faaaamily'. Although they can appear tough it doesn't take much to get a Cancerian crying and once they start they can't stop; they will blub if their daughter-in-law refuses to come for Sunday lunch, but the rock hard side of them will secretly curse the 'nasty bitch'.

They like the finer things in life, but can be quite lazy, so the idea of leaving the house and actually going out and grafting for a living doesn't really appeal; they are not averse to making easy (illegal) money, Cancerians are physically the most identifiable of the Zodiac signs, as they often have enormous arses from sitting on their backsides all day.

Wendy suggests:
WIFE OF MAFIA BOSS
BENEFIT FRAUDSTER
ACTRESS

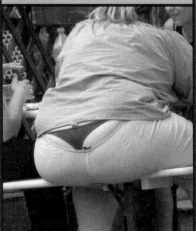

Leo

QUEEN OF THE JUNGLE

Possibly the most intelligent of the star signs (certainly in their opinion), the Leonine woman has great self belief and thinks she can do anything, especially when it involves her issuing orders and other people completing the task. As she likes to be both the boss and in the spotlight, jobs that offer a podium and a platform for her views are preferable. It's no surprise then that becoming a magistrate is, for many of them, a liftime's ambition (they are also quite keen wig wearers).

Telling people what to do is their favourite thing in the whole wide world and the idea of summoning people to their office is enough to give most Leos a spine-busting orgasm. What they have to remember is that there is a fine line between strictness and bullying and that corporal punishment was outlawed on the British mainland in the seventies. As the star sign with the most S&M freaks, they are better off leaving their 'little light beatings' to the bedroom.

Wendy suggests:
HEAD MISTRESS
SUPERVISOR
DOMINATRIX

Virgo

THE PRISSY VIRGIN

 The tidiest of all the star signs, Virgoans are also the least sexy and most worried about having too many buttons undone.

Being a 'neat freak' can have its compensations and Virgoans are quite happy in mindless repetitive jobs that would have other people screaming within minutes. Things like alphabetical filing or making sure that edges are straight are deeply satisfying for those who often hide the fact that their tidyness has slipped into some sort of obsessive compulsion.

Possibly the most servile of the signs, they are in great demand as personal assistants and can be trusted with keys and important papers, and not letting the boss forget his wife's birthday. The wives will approve as even when the Virgoan secretary takes her glasses off and lets down her hair, she is still rather plain.

Wendy suggests:
SECRETARY
CHARITY WORKER
CHAMBERMAID

Wendy's Jobs For Girls

★ JOBS TO SUIT YOUR STAR SIGN ★

Libra

THE FAIR-MINDED DITHERER

Librans are quite nice. which really means they're a bit dull. Something like 87% of Librans have never shoplifted anything in their lives, not even an eye-shadow pencil or a small bar of chocolate. For this reason they can be trusted with jobs like working a till. However, some of them are quite bright and, being legally minded, will naturally gravitate to the Law or the social services; they are born to take decisions regarding children who are born to be chain-smoking, ass-scratching crisp-eaters.

The biggest Libran character flaw is their ability to pretend to agree with both sides of an argument. They flaunt their reputation as the Zodiac's peace-keepers but they're actually a bit two-faced, which is why the really clever ones become solicitors.

Many Librans can suffer from depression on realising the world is not as fair as they imagined. They also suffer from kidney troubles and urinary tract infections, so they really need a job where they can regularly visit the loo.

Wendy suggests:
CHILDRENS WELFARE OFFICER
SOLICITOR
LAVATORY ATTENDANT

Scorpio

THE EXOTIC INSECT WITH THE POISONOUS STING

The most dangerous and slightly scary of all of the star signs, Scorpians tend to 'make it' by making sure that other people don't. Naturally aggressive, and amoral, the characters of the world of politics are mere children compared to the manipulative pushy monster that is your average Scorpian. She will not rest until she rules the world, or is at least in charge of the IT department.

Scorpians are quite dressy and tend to look good in power suits, so they've been waiting for an eighties revival for twenty years and secretly worship Margaret Thatcher. Trenchcoats do them wonders, so spying is always an option and, as they like to play mind games, psychotherapy is something they could toy with, even though they know it's all poppycock. Scorpian women should never be allowed to work with small children or the frail and elderly as they can often be quite cruel. Interesting fact: there are more Scorpian muderesses in prison than any other star sign. Well, it was interesting to us.

Wendy suggests:
WORLD LEADER
SPY
SHRINK
KILLER

Sagittarius

THE SYBARITIC ARCHER

In some respects, the most self-indulgent of all the star signs, Sagittarians can be wilfully childish and incapable of adult responsibility. Hopeless with authority and incapable of understanding why they have to pay tax, most of them are excused because they don't earn enough to warrant it. Many Sagittarians have a Mother Earth complex, are somewhat hippyish, and are consequently overweight – too much hash cake. Despite being the chubbiest of the zodiac, they often want to be dancers but then they also refuse to cut their hair and claim to be able to read tea leaves. They are a confused people. Most Sagittarians would be happy working on a fairground or in the circus, and occasionally they can make a living out of folk singing – but not a proper grown up living.

Wendy suggests:
SPIRTUALIST
FRAUDSTER
(FAT) DANCER

WHAT DO YOUR SLIPPERS SAY ABOUT YOU?

Our Resident Mister Style-ista, POISON IVAN runs his razor-sharp eyeballs over your indoor footwear

TOWELLING SLIP ON STOLEN FROM SPA HOTEL

Who do you think you are, Catherine Zeta Jones? This is the slipper for the woman who likes to show off the fact she's wearing nail varnish on her toes – how shallow, we've all had the occasional pamper day at a Spa love, but not all of us feel we have to steal the merchandise. As Paris Hilton always says 'True class is not bothering to touch the freebies'.

NOVELTY CARTOON MONSTERS

Eurgh and double eurgh, when are you going to learn that slippers like this are neither stylish nor safe? When you fall over them walking downstairs and break your neck, that's when!

So the kids got you them for Xmas, this is no excuse, in fact it only goes to show that you have genetically burdened your children with appalling taste. Eurgh, I bet you've all got matching tracksuits and eat own label crisps.

TRADITIONAL WITH POM POM

Now you're either in your eighties and caught in a kind of weird Miss Marple style groove, all pleated skirts and lace blouses with cameo brooches – in which case that's kind of cool in a retro, lady detective way. Or you're a cutting edge, achingly Kate Moss-style fashionista – pom poms are ironic, in fact the only way to wear your pom pom slippers is naked whilst licking vodka from the belly button of your rock star boyfriend – unless you're over fifty, in which case do us all a favour – just wear them whilst you're dipping ginger nuts in a cup of milky tea.

SOME WOVEN ETHNIC/NORDIC FELT/CHINESE EMROIDERED THINGS

Think we're a bit of a maverick do we, are slippers a bit suburban for you, are you raging against the machine? Are you desperate for someone to say, 'Gosh, those are unusual slippers', so that you can bore them with stories about your trek through Mongolia and how the people are really spiritual and how you bought your slippers from a woman who knitted them out of yak hair, only she didn't really, they're made in a factory in Pontypridd.

THOSE SOCK THINGS WITH NON SLIP SOLES

These are for people who live in dread of slipping on a laminate floor, ideal for the nervous type with a skidding phobia – as they're a bit like wearing mini-bath mats under your feet – and just as attractive. The trouble with the under-foot suction slipper sock is that the suction pads tend to pick up a good deal of dirt and grease rendering them very grubby indeed. In fact the one good thing about these slippers is that just by walking around your house you can tell if the cleaner has really done her job: if the soles are covered in jam and hair – sack the lazy cow.

ODE TO OLD LADIES

Here at *Wendy* we sometimes receive readers' letters that get the whole office laughing, or talking or, in this case, sobbing uncontrollably, and we have taken the unusual step of printing the letter to the right in full to cut out and keep. That way you can send it to your daughter or daughter-in-law, or son when they fail to call you often enough or forget your birthday. It might just work.

All of a sudden I look at old ladies in a different way. Instead of being irritated by them or finding them maddeningly slow when they get to the till at Tesco's, all of a sudden I want to rush up to them and give them a great big hug.

One minute she was sitting by the hospital bed with her best dressing gown and nightie on, asking me to bring in her reading glasses and some arrowroot biscuits – and the next minute she goes and dies. I hadn't had time to say goodbye, to tell her all the things I wanted to, to remember all the things only she and I would remember, like how we used to sit underneath the dining room table with some cushions and listen to <u>Listen with Mother</u> after lunch and play dens, or how much we both hated Mrs Hargreaves the ballet teacher that day she said I had weak ankles.

I was always so stupidly busy, fitting in a quick visit or call to her between work and kids and shopping and friends, never really giving her the time and attention she deserved. Not that she ever complained to me. She was always thinking of me instead – 'I don't want you setting off in the dark, you get back to your girls' – and now all the opportunities to talk to her, to make it up to her, to hug her even, have gone.

I feel like I have lost my deepest anchor, the person who in so many ways defined and steadied me. I wasn't prepared. I thought I was my own woman, that I was so different to her in my values and outlook that her death would be painful but wouldn't challenge my own existence. How wrong I was. How could I have been prepared? Now, every scrap of her is precious: her photos, the things she kept in the

EVERYWHERE

drawer, her dressing gown that still smells of her, letters that she wrote to my father in the war that I hadn't seen before, birthday cards she kept I had sent her, even the arrowroot biscuits, all of these things feel like the only opportunity I now have to value her, to take my time and luxuriate in her in the way that I wish I had when she was here, knowing as I do know that as time goes on these small objects will become the all important triggers of her memory and so will become her, what she now is.

Now she's gone I realise that my mother taught me everything I know, not the fancy stuff, not my education or how to read a map – no, she taught me the important stuff – how to get tea on the table within thirty minutes of getting through the door, put a wash on, empty the dishwasher and iron a shirt all at the same time. Most importantly she taught me how to love well. How to look after someone who's poorly, or take them a hot water bottle to make them feel cosy, or lay them a little tray with a boiled egg and a flower on, or to tuck them up in bed and kiss their forehead. she knew me better than anyone else is likely ever to know me, deeply, scarily, uncritically, I suppose unrealistically. And now there is no one to tell my little triumphs to, knowing that she would be invariably chuffed and proud, no one to send the kids' school photos to, no one to ask about Great Uncle Albert or what happened to Aunty Beattie's wedding ring.

Audrey Brown
Recently orphaned at 54
Peterborough

PROBLEM PAGE

Got something on your mind? Don't let it gnaw away like a rat chewing on a mouldy pigeon carcass, get it off your chest and let Glenda and Derek Parnell come to the rescue. Glenda and Derek have been married for thirty years and what they don't know about dull sex, extra-marital relationships, prescription-drug dependency, financial difficulties and the disappointment that having children brings isn't worth knowing.

Dear Glenda and Derek,
I get confused between CDs and DVDs. What's the difference? Also, can you put an STD in a laptop?
Confused of Ipswich

Derek: Of course you can, you silly billy.
Glenda: Don't listen to Derek, he doesn't know what he's talking about. If I were you I'd get down to the nearest G.U.M clinic and get yourself sorted out.

Dear Glenda and Derek,
Why can't there be some sort of promise to pro-vide decent packed lunches in the wedding vows? I've been married for fifteen years and the contents of my packed lunches have deteriorated badly despite promising beginnings. I feel badly let down.
Yours hungrily
Nigel Plinth, (aged 46), Poulten Le Fylde

Glenda: Make your own.
Derek: Yes, otherwise you will find yourself fainting at work as I did last Thursday.

Dear G and D,
I keep having rude dreams about my daughter's boyfriend. Should I hand myself in to the police?
Margot from Solihull

Derek: Whoa, before you go handing yourself in to the police, just remember you haven't actually done anything wrong (have you?) and so far it's all in your head. Whatever you do, keep these dreams to yourself. However, if you do get the urge to touch his hair or brush past him in the kitchen, then it might be sensible to put yourself out of harm's way and emigrate.
Glenda: Can you send me a photo?

Dear Glenda and Derek,
I have fallen out with my best friend and need your expertise in help-ing us settle an argument. Was it Mary Hopkin or Dana who sang 'All Kinds of Everything'? I say Dana but my friend Brenda says Mary Hopkin. Please tell me she's wrong.
Yours, Deidre Ogle, Littlehampton

Glenda: What does it matter, they were both really rub-bish. Might it not be time to do some voluntary work?
Derek: I'm pretty sure it was Dana, the lovely Irish Eu-rovision singing sensation. Voice that could charm the birds from the trees.

Dear Glenda and Derek,
Do you think it's ever acceptable to buy shoes from the chemist's?
Yours Avril (bunion sufferer), Nantwich

Derek: Avril, you're talking Dr Scholl here aren't you? Well, rejoice, there's no shame now in orthopaedic foot-wear, and thanks to some snazzy new designs, rubber soles are all the rage.
Glenda: Actually I beg to differ. It's better that your feet should bleed than ever resort to matron shoes.

Dear Glenda and Derek,
My best friend and I are both interested in the same divorced fella who belongs to our bridge club. My friend has taken to wearing revealing low-cut tops and red lipstick and she's making a show of herself. Should I tell her that people are starting to talk about her behind her back?
Betty Luttock, Staffordshire

Glenda: Are you sure it's not just you talking about her behind her back? Come on misery guts, get your bumpy bits out, lash on a bit of lippy – you know what they say, if you can't beat them, why not act the slut too? Who knows, one of you might be pregnant by Christmas!
Derek: Yes, but make sure if you are having sex, it's in a loving relationship.
Glenda: Precisely why Derek and I stopped having sex.

Dear Glenda and Derek,
I keep having filthy dreams about Phillip Schofield. Is this normal and do you think his wife would mind if I left a small token of my affection, such as a potted plant on his doorstep?
Norma Beetham, Gravesend

Derek: We think she'd be touched, but just make sure the plant isn't anything silly – a small lobelia might be just the ticket.
Glenda: Filthy dreams about other men can often be a sign that your own relationship is in trouble. Last night I dreamt I had sex, doggy-style, in a Travel Lodge just outside of Nuneaton with the England rugby hero, Jonny Wilkinson.

Dear Glenda and Derek,
I shared a packed lunch with a coach driver on a trip to a place of historical interest and ever since I've felt a bit queasy and bloated. Might I be pregnant?
Anon, Reading

Derek: Depends on the sandwich filling! Only joking. The only way you could be pregnant is if you were having sexual intercourse whilst eating the sandwich, which is highly unlikely as we know how popular coach trips are and it's doubtful you were alone together on the coach. If you're still not sure, ask your friends. Maybe one of them noticed you having sex with the driver and it's just slipped your mind.
Glenda: I bet you did. Coach trips are so dull; the only way of livening them up is to have sex with the driver.

Dear Glenda and Derek,
I am fed up with my best friend; she keeps borrowing things and not giving them back. First it was my blender, then my Cranford DVD, and now to crown it, she's only gone and borrowed my husband and I haven't seen him since Tuesday week. Should I send her a polite note reminding her that it's time I got my bits and Bob back?
Joanne Ruttle, Kidderminster

Glenda: Hmm, I think it's a bit late for polite notes. Maybe it's high time you went round there and caused a scene; after all Bob is your husband. If she won't give him back then an ombudsman should be able to retrieve your other goods.
Derek: Or the ombobsman could get him back!
Glenda: It's because Derek makes jokes like this that I am divorcing him.

OH GOODIE, AN EXCUSE TO PRINT ANOTHER PIC OF PHIILLIP SCHOLFIELD - HOORAH!

MORE PROBLEMS

Dear Glenda and Derek,

My grandchildren are really dull. All my friends have got really interesting grandchildren but mine are hopeless. They never win or do anything.

Embarrassed Gran, Nottingham

Derek: Really E.G. it's a granny's job to love their grandchildren unconditionally. After all, you don't want them to grow up with all sorts of complexes that could lead to self-harming in the future.

Glenda: Listen E.G., all grandchildren are dull. It's your job as a nana to make them sound more exciting than they really are. All you need to do is lie through your teeth about their achievements, that's what everyone else does. For example, Derek's grandma told everyone he was an Olympic ice skater because she couldn't bear the embarrassment of having such a wuss for a grandson.

Dear Glenda and Derek,

We have recently come back from a family holiday in Majorca and our 14-year-old daughter has been attracting a lot of unwelcome attraction from men. Wolf whistles and even notes from our table waiter asking her to go out for a drink! Can you suggest something that we could do to avoid the same situation on our next holiday?

Concerned Mum, Plymouth

Glenda: I think a lot of readers will identify with this very common problem. There is one quick and easy solution. You need to get her referred to your local orthodontist and get her fixed up with the kind of brace that looks like it might double as a waste disposal unit or outboard motor. Hey presto, no more unwelcome advances! And the nice thing is it's going to make you look that bit better at the same time! It's win-win.

Derek: I think readers should know that Glenda and our daughter have been estranged for a number of years.

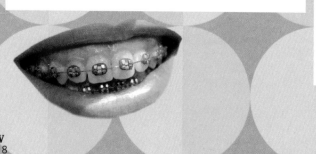

Dear Glenda and Derek,

I thought at my age I would have grown out of silly crushes, but I find myself strongly attracted to Norman, who swims in the middle lane at the early birds' swim session. I even find myself blushing and making sure that I'm in the water in time for when he arrives (wouldn't want him to see me waddling over to the water - best to be neck deep). He hasn't spoken to me yet, but I am worried he will think me too forward if I strike up a conversation with him and after all he would have to take off his nose clips.

Yours girlishly,

Yellow swimming hat, Gwent

Derek: You need a way of gaining his attention, but on no account should you pal up with the torso used for mouth-to-mouth that sits on the side of the pool – this will only make you look like a madwoman and is likely to backfire. Although many women do find grabbing hold of one and swimming with it while holding hands is useful if the lane you are in is horribly busy. Have you noticed whether he wears glasses on dry land? If so, why worry about looking a little podgy on the poolside – you'll be a blurry misty blob to him once he gets those nose clips and goggles on anyway. Think positive.

Glenda: Actually Norma, Derek can't swim. I, on the other hand, used to compete for the county.

Dear Glenda and Derek,

You're probably thinking what's a bloke writing in for? The thing is, my wife has gone very moody of late, keeps going round slamming doors and complaining about being too hot. Our last daughter left home recently and she has put on quite a lot of weight. Do you think this could be the reason for her bad temper? She is fifty-two and a size sixteen.

Yours

Kevin Hendon, The Potting Shed, Swindon

Derek: Kevin, she's menopausal you idiot. Stand well back and don't say anything stupid in the kitchen when she's got a sharp knife.

Glenda: And for God's sake, tell her she looks more like a 14 than a 16.

Dear Glenda and Derek
My wife is very sociable and likes going to parties. I can't stand them, do I have to go?
Yours, Norman, Lancs.

Derek: Maybe you should compromise and both of you go, but just for a short time. Make it a condition that if you accompany her then you want to be home by ten.

Glenda: Norman, why don't you let your wife go by herself? With any luck she will meet someone a bit more fun and have a really fabulous affair whilst you sit at home in front of the telly – your choice, mate.

Dear Glenda and Derek,

I have been concerned for some time about my daughter who seems to spend an awful lot of her time writing in her diary, and I have always said that since my own mother used to spy on my own diary I would never do such a thing. However, while dusting her room this morning I accidentally dusted it on to the floor, the lock broke and it fell open. I found myself unable to control the urge to read it. I don't know what came over me . . .

Kay Jolly, (not my real name, obviously), Micklehampton

Glenda: You seem determined to look at your teen-age children's secrets and are going about it in a way which is irritating for two reasons: a) it's twee and silly to pretend you don't really want to see it, and b) there is a much easier way of doing it. Haven't you even heard of Facebook and Bebo? Just go on and register your own page and you will be able to get on to theirs, see their latest photos, social arrangements, liaisons and all kinds of things they don't want you to know about. For this to work properly you must not blow your cover – it's crucial to pretend you are a computer luddite. Also, while you're busy doing your important daily snooping, you could also join one of the squillions of middle-aged dating clubs on the internet. That's where all the action is these days.

Derek: Yes, that's where Glenda met Sergio.

Glenda: And Wolfgang and Nick.

Dear Glenda and Derek,
My husband and I will be celebrating our thirtieth wedding anniversary in a few months. Unfortunately, we seem to have fallen out over the catering plans. I say tapas, he says nada – actually we haven't said anything since this disagreement and he has moved into the shed. Do you think I should go ahead with the party and if so, should I invite him?
Roberta Chamberlain, Stoke Newington, London

Derek: Before you do anything drastic ask yourself is it really worth throwing thirty years of marriage down the pan for the sake of some smelly chorizo and a bit of cold frittata?

Glenda: Of course it is! If he won't do what you want, get rid of him. Turn the party into an end of thirty years of marriage celebration. Do it however you like, go Spanish crazy and get a great big piñata in the shape of his head. Arriba!

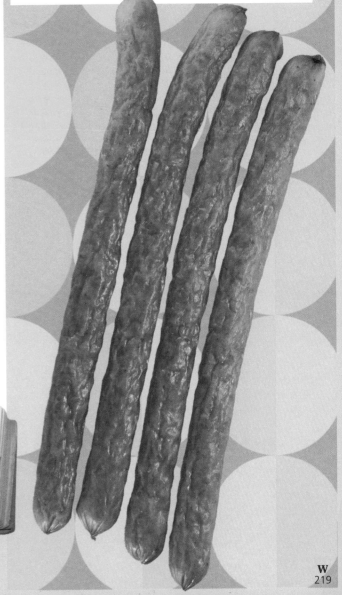

Dreamy
Days

Ashamed about reading chic lit in public?

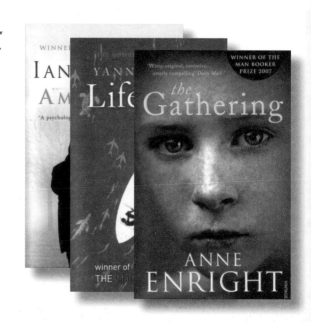

You should be. Cover your embarrassing book club choice with one of these handy Booker prize-winning jackets.

THE TOO LATE TO LEARN CENTRE presents...

The Fake Blackberry

For the elderly retired executive who can't be bothered with new-fangled gadgetry but still likes to look the part, the fake blackberry looks like the real thing, makes authentic noises, and even breaks down as often. It just doesn't require any technical ability whatsoever.

Suitable for the over-seventies or the luddite of any age.

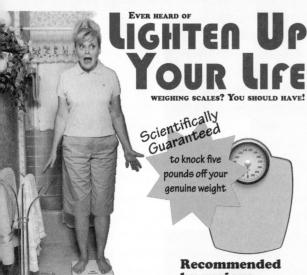

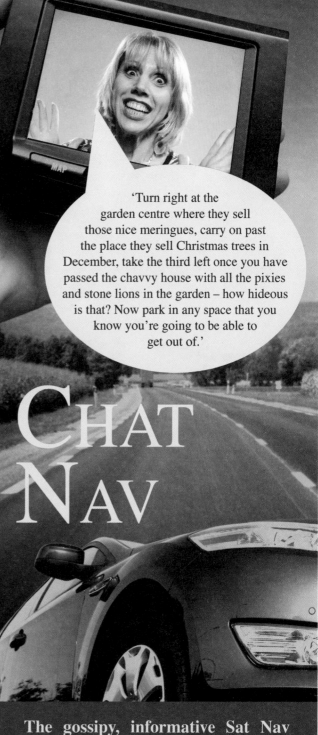

'Wendy' photographed by Adrian Franklin
Most illustrations by Marcus Reed

Photographic credits (t = top, b = bottom, l = left, r = right, c = centre)

Alamy: 28, 32, 34 cl, 49 b, 51 tr, 54 t, 68 br, 69 br, 71 tr, 88, 91 t, 119 tl, 127 b, 129 b, 142 tl, 143, 159 tl, 161 b, 162, 164 r, 165 l, 165 t, 166 t, 169 cr, 169 tr, 171, 175 b, 198r, 199b, 211 tl, 219. Corbis: 91 br, 186-187 t, 189 c. Food Features: 77. Getty Images: 10 tr, 16 bl, 16 tl, 17 tl, 31 br, 34, 35 bl, 38 tl, 38 tl, 39 l, 51 cr, 52, 53, 71 br, 71 cl, 72 l, 82 b, 119 c, 119 cr, 121 b, 124, 125, 126 l, 127 t, 128 b, 133 tr, 137 bc, 137 bl, 145, 148, 156, 159 tr, 161 t, 163 r, 165 b, 166, 169 cl, 175 c, 188 t, 194, 195 l, 198 l, 199 r, 202, 212 l, 212 r, 221 bl, 221 tl, 221 tr. The Kobal Collection/Columbia: 16 bl. The Kobal Collection/Tambarle/ Compact Yellowbill: 139b. Photolibrary.com: 140. Redcover.com/Smith/Honky Design: 218. Rex Features: 8 l, 9 r, 10 bl, 10 br, 11 bl, 16 tr, 24, 25, 26 t, 27 b, 33 b, 34 br, 34 c, 35 c, 35 tl, 35 tr, 40 – 41, 41 b, 41 t, 44 l, 45 bl, 46 t, 48, 50, 54 b, 55, 71 cr, 71 tl, 86, 87, 90 l, 117 br, 117 tr, 118 c, 124, 125, 132 br, 132 tr, 134, 135l, 135r, 137 br, 137 t, 142 bl, 142 c, 150 br, 151 b, 154, 155, 158 b, 172, 173, 174, 205, 209 tr, 211 b, 217, 221 c. Endpapers: Getty Images/Rex Features.

Every reasonable effort has been made to trace copyright holders, but if there are any errors or omissions, Hodder & Stoughton will be pleased to insert the appropriate acknowledgement in any subsequent edition.

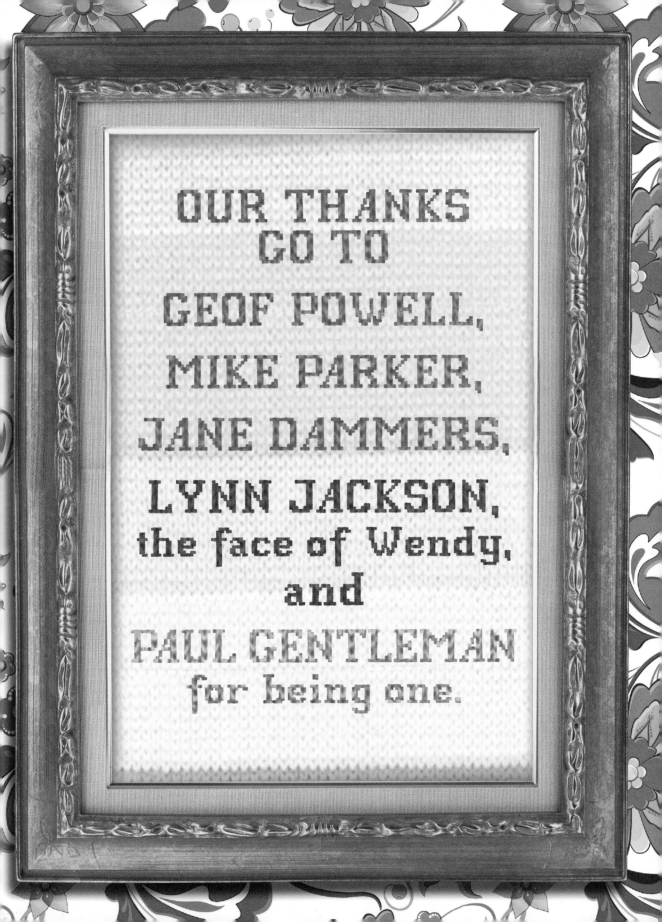

OUR THANKS
GO TO

GEOF POWELL,

MIKE PARKER,

JANE DAMMERS,

LYNN JACKSON,
the face of Wendy,
and

PAUL GENTLEMAN
for being one.